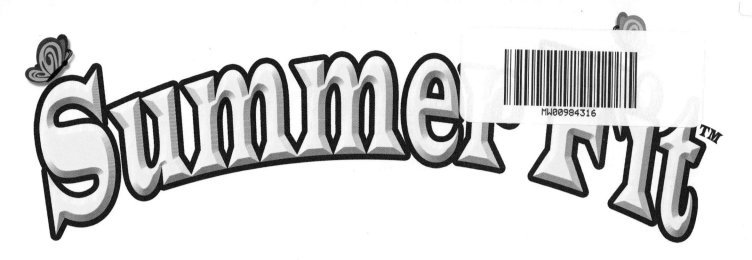

"I pledge to be active this summer, to be kind to myself, and to others."

_____
Name

20____
Year

Let's Get Ready for Fourth Grade!

Summer Fit Third to Fourth Grade

Authors: Kelly Terrill and Sarria James

Fitness and Nutrition: Lisa Roberts RN, BSN, PHN, James Cordova, Charles Miller, Steve Edwards, Missy Jones, Barbara Sherwood, John Bartlette, Malu Egido, Michael Ward

Healthy Family Lifestyle: Jay and Jen Jacobs & Marci and Courtney Crozier

Layout and Design: Scott Aucutt

Cover Design and Illustrations: Andy Carlson

Illustrations: Roxanne Ottley and Scott Aucutt

Series Created by George Starks

Summer Fit Dedication

Summer Fit is dedicated to Julia Hobbs and Carla Fisher who are the authors and unsung heroes of the original summer workbook series that helped establish the importance of summer learning. These women helped pioneer summer learning and dedicated their lives to teaching children and supporting parents. Carla and Julia made the world a better place by touching the lives of others using their love of education.

Summer Fit is also dedicated to Michael Starks whose presence is missed dearly, but who continues to teach us every day the importance of having courage in difficult times and treating others with respect, dignity, and a genuine concern for others.

Summer Fit Caution

If you have any questions regarding your child's ability to complete any of the suggested fitness activities consult your family doctor or child's pediatrician. Some of these exercises may require adult supervision. Children should stretch and warm up before exercises. Do not push children past their comfort level or ability. These physical fitness activities were created to be fun for parents and caregivers as well as the child, but not as a professional training or weight loss program. Exercise should stop immediately if you or your child experiences any of the following symptoms: pain, feeling dizzy or faint, nausea, or severe fatigue.

Summer Fit Copyright

Special thanks to the Terry Fox Foundation for use of Terry's photo and inspiring us all to contribute to making the world a better place for others each in our own way.

Printed in the USA
All Rights Reserved
ISBN: 978-0-9762800-4-0
www.SummerFitLearning.com

TABLE OF CONTENTS

Importance of Summer Learning and Fitness

Dear Parents,

Without opportunities to learn and practice essential skills over the summer months, most children fall behind academically. Research shows that summer learning loss varies, but that children can lose the equivalency of 2.5 months of math and 2 months of reading skills while away from school. In addition, children lose more than just academic knowledge during the summer. Research also shows that children are at greater risk of actually gaining more weight during summer vacation than during the school year:

All young people experience learning losses when they do not engage in educational activities during the summer. Research spanning 100 years shows that students typically score lower on standardized tests at the end of summer vacation than they do on the same tests at the beginning of the summer (White, 1906; Heyns, 1978; Entwisle & Alexander 1992; Cooper, 1996; Downey et al, 2004).

Research shows that children gain weight three times faster during the summer months – gaining as much weight during the summer as they do during the entire school year – even though the summertime is three times shorter. Von Hippel, P. T., Powell, B., Downey, D.B., & Rowland, N. (2007).

In the New York City school system, elementary and middle school students who placed in the top third of a fitness scale had better math and reading scores than students in the bottom third of the fitness scale. Those who were in the top 5% for fitness scored an average of 36 percentage points higher on state reading and math exams than did the least-fit 5%. New York City Department of Health. (2009)

Summer vacation is a great opportunity to use a variety of resources and programs to extend the academic learning experience and to reinforce life and social skills. It is an opportunity to give learning a different look and feel than what children are used to during the school year. Summer is a season that should be fun and carefree, but do not underestimate the opportunity and importance of helping children prepare for the upcoming school year. The key to a successful new school year is keeping your children active and learning this summer!

Sincerely,

Summer Fit Learning

FACT
You are your child's greatest teacher.

Inside Summer Fit

Purpose

The purpose of Summer Fit is to offer a comprehensive program for parents that promotes health and physical activity along side of academic and social skills. Summer Fit is designed to help create healthy and balanced family lifestyles.

Stay Smart

Summer Fit contains activities in reading, writing, math, language arts, science, and geography.

Program Components

Summer Fit activities and exercises are divided into 10 sections to correlate with the traditional 10 weeks of summer. Each section begins with a weekly overview and incentive calendar so parents and children can talk about the week ahead while reviewing the previous week. There are 10 pages of activities for each week. The child does 2 pages a day that should take 20-30 minutes a day to complete. Each day offers a simple routine to reinforce basic skills and includes a physical fitness exercise and healthy habit. Each week also reinforces a core value on a daily basis to build character and social skills. Activities start off easy and progressively get more difficult so by the end of the workbook children are mentally, physically and socially prepared for the grade ahead.

Stay Cool

Summer Fit uses core value activities and role models to reinforce the importance of good character and social skills.

Stay Active

Summer Fit uses a daily fitness exercise and wellness tips to keep children moving and having fun.

Summer Fit includes a daily exercise program that children complete as part of their one-page of activities a day. These daily exercises and movement activities foster active lifestyles and get parents and children moving together.

Summer Fit uses daily value-based activities to reinforce good behavior.

Summer Fit promotes the body-brain connection and gives parents the tools to motivate children to use both.

Summer Fit includes an online component that gives children and parents additional summer learning and fitness resources at SummerFitLearning.com.

Summer Fit contains activities and exercises created by educators, parents and trainers committed to creating active learning environments that include movement and play as part of the learning experience.

Summer Fit uses role models from around the world to introduce and reinforce core values and the importance of good behavior.

Teaching the Whole Child

The Whole Child philosophy is based on the belief that every child should be healthy, engaged, supported and challenged in all aspects of their lives. Investing in the *overall* development of your child is critical to their personal health and well being. There is increased awareness that a balanced approach to nurturing and teaching our children will benefit all aspects of their lives; therefore creating well rounded students who are better equipped to successfully navigate the ups and downs of their education careers.

Supports Common Core Standards

The Common Core provides teachers and parents with a common understanding of what students are expected to learn. These standards will provide appropriate benchmarks for all students, regardless of where they live and be applied for students in grades K-12. Summer Fit is aligned to Common Core Standards.

Learn more at: CoreStandards.org

Top 5 Parent Summer Tips

1 Routine: Set a time and a place for your child to complete their activities and exercises each day.

2 Balance: Use a combination of resources to reinforce basics skills in fun ways. Integrate technology with traditional learning, but do not replace one with another.

3 Motivate and Encourage: Inspire your child to complete their daily activities and exercises. Get excited and show your support of their accomplishments!

4 Play as a Family: Slap "high 5," jump up and down and get silly! Show how fun it is to be active by doing it yourself! Health Experts recommend 60 minutes of play a day and kids love seeing parents playing and having fun!

5 Eat Healthy (and together): Kids are more likely to eat less healthy during the summer, than during the school year. Put food back on the table and eat together at least once a day.

Health and Wellness in the Home

Physical activity is critical to your child's health and well-being. Research shows that children with better health are in school more days, learn better, have higher self esteem and lower risk of developing chronic diseases.

Exercise Provides:

✔ Stronger muscles and bones

✔ Leaner body because exercise helps control body fat

✔ Increased blood flow to the brain and wellness at home

✔ Lower blood pressure and blood cholesterol levels

✔ Kids who are active are less likely to develop weight issues, display more self-confidence, perform better academically and enjoy a better overall quality of life!

Tips from a former *Biggest Loser*

Jay Jacobs
Former contestant of NBC's
The Biggest Loser

Jay Jacobs lost 181 pounds on Season 11 of NBC's *The Biggest Loser*.

Sedentary lifestyles, weight issues and unhealthy habits need to be addressed at home. It is more likely that your child will include healthy habits as part of their everyday life if they understand:

✔ Why staying active and eating healthy is important

✔ What are healthy habits and what are not

✔ How to be healthy, active and happy

Go to the Health and Wellness Index in the back of the book for more Family Health and Wellness Tips.

Warm Up!

It is always best to prepare your body for any physical activity by moving around and stretching.

Get Loose! Stretch!

Move your head from side to side, trying to touch each shoulder. Now move your head forward, touching your chin to your chest and then looking up and back as far as you can, trying to touch your back with the back of your head.

Touch your toes when standing, bend over at the waist and touch the end of your toes or the floor. Hold this for 10 seconds.

Get Moving

Walk or jog for 3-5 minutes to warm up before you exercise. Shake your arms and roll your shoulders when you are finished walking or jogging.

Healthy Eating and Nutrition

A healthy diet and daily exercise will maximize the likelihood of children growing up healthy and strong. Children are still growing and adding bone mass, so a balanced diet is very important to their overall health. Provide three nutritious meals a day that include fruits and vegetables. Try to limit fast food consumption, and find time to cook more at home where you know the source of your food and how your food is prepared. Provide your child with healthy, well-portioned snacks, and try to keep them from eating too much at a time.

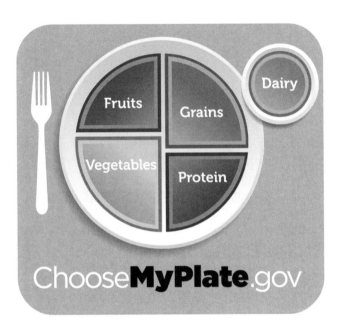

SCORE! A HEALTHY EATING GOAL

As a rule of thumb, avoid foods and drinks that are high in sugars, fat, or caffeine. Try to provide fruits, vegetables, grains, lean meats, chicken, fish, and low-fat dairy products as part of a healthy meal when possible. Obesity and being overweight, even in children, can significantly increase the risk of heart disease, diabetes, and other chronic illnesses. Creating an active lifestyle this summer that includes healthy eating and exercise will help your child maintain a healthy weight and protect them from certain illnesses throughout the year.

Let's Eat Healthy!

5 Steps to Improve Eating Habits of Your Family

1) Make fresh fruits and veggies readily available.

2) Cook more at home, and sit down for dinner as a family.

3) Limit consumption of soda, desserts and sugary cereals.

4) Serve smaller portions.

5) Limit snacks to just one or two daily.

Technology and Child Development

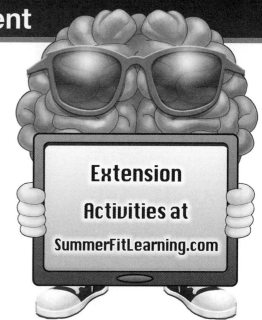

Children start developing initiative and creativity at a young age. Technology offers children additional outlets to learn and demonstrate their creativity. However, it is critical that active playtime and traditional learning resources are included as an essential part of the child's daily routine in addition to technology use. Used appropriately, computers can be a positive element of children's play and learning as they explore and experiment. Screen time (including TV, computer, phone and games) should be limited to a maximum of one to two hours per day for young children (American Academy of Pediatrics). High Screen time is associated with a more sedentary life style and excess snacking.

Extension Activities at SummerFitLearning.com

3 KEYS TO TECH SUCCESS

1 Consider technology as one tool among many used to enhance learning, not as a replacement for child interactions with each other, with adults, or other modes of learning.

2 Explore touch screens with a wide variety of appropriate interactive media experiences with your child. Verbally communicate with them the concepts of the game or apps that engage them. Express interest and encouragement of their performance.

3 Establish "No Screen Zones" for children such as the dinner table at home and in public settings. Screens create barriers that are difficult to talk through and can easily isolate children and parents. Establishing appropriate times and places to use technology will help children develop "tech-etiquette."

Core Values in the Home

Understanding core values allows your child to have a clearer understanding of their own behavior in your home, in their classroom and in our communities. Core values are fundamental to society and are incorporated into our civil laws, but are taught first and foremost at home. Parents and guardians are the most important and influential people in a child's life. It is up to you to raise children who respect and accept themselves, and others around them.

Role Models

A role model is a person who serves as an example of a particular value or trait. There are many people today, and throughout history, who exemplify in their own actions the values that we strive to have ourselves, and teach our children.

Mother Teresa
Winner of the
Nobel Prize

Rosa Parks
Advocate for
civil rights

Bullying

In recent years, bullying has become a leading topic of concern. It is a complex issue, and can be difficult for parents to know what to do when they hear that their child is being bullied or is bullying others. Bullying is always wrong. It is critical that you intervene appropriately when bullying occurs. Make sure your child understands what bullying means. Check in with your child often to make sure he/she knows you are interested and aware of what is going on in their social lives.

Learn more at StopBullying.gov

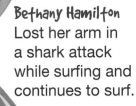

Bethany Hamilton
Lost her arm in a shark attack while surfing and continues to surf.

Books Build Better Brains!

Reading is considered the gateway to all learning, so it is critical as a parent or caregiver to assist and encourage children to read at all grade levels regardless of reading ability.

1. Create a daily reading routine. A reading routine provides the practice a child needs to reinforce and build reading and literacy skills.

2. Create a summer reading list. Choose a variety of children's books, including fairy tales, poems, fiction and non-fiction books.

3. Join or start a summer reading club. Check your local public library or bookstore.

4. Talk with your child about a book that you are reading. Let your child see how much you enjoy reading and ask them to share stories from some of their favorite books.

5. Children love to hear stories about their family. Tell your child what it was like when you or your parents were growing up, or talk about a funny thing that happened when you were their age. Have them share stories of their own about when they were "young."

Read 20 minutes a day!

CYBER READERS: Books in a Digital World

With the amount of electronic resources available, children are gaining access to subjects faster than ever before. With electronic resources comes a significant amount of "screen time" that children spend with technology including television, movies, computers, phones and gaming systems. It is important to manage "screen time" and include time for books. Reading a book helps develop attention spans and allows children to build their imaginations without the aid of animated graphics, special effects and sound that may hinder a child's ability to create these for themselves.

Summer Reading List – Third to Fourth Grade

Color the  for every title read and the **Book Report activity page** (in the back of the book) is completed. Go to SummerFitLearning.com to download and print out more **Book Report activity pages** to complete.

Reading is the gateway to all learning and by third grade it is critical that your child is reading at grade level. This is because third grade is the year that students move from learning to read - decoding words using their knowledge of the alphabet - to reading to learn.

Children who have not made the leap to fast, fluent reading begin at this moment to fall behind. Keep your child reading this summer to help ensure mastery of reading skills

☆ **The Wizard of Oz**
By Baum, L. Frank

☆ **Tales of a Fourth Grade Nothing**
By Blume, Judy

☆ **The Pinballs**
By Byars, Betsy

☆ **Ramona Quimby, Age Eight**
By Cleary, Beverly

☆ **Charlie and the Chocolate Factory**
By Dahl, Roald

☆ **Garfield Counts to Ten**
By Davis, Jim

☆ **Nothing's Fair in Fifth Grade**
By DeClements, Barthe

☆ **The Black Stallion**
By Farley, Walter.

☆ **The Great Brain**
By Fitzgerald, John D

☆ **Old Yeller**
By Gipson, Fred

☆ **The Karate Kid**
By Hiller, B.B.

☆ **Bunnicula: A Rabbit Tale of Mystery**
By Howe, Deborah and James

☆ **The Lion, the Witch, and the Wardrobe**
By Lewis, C.S.

☆ **Island of the Blue Dolphins**
By O'Dell, Scott

☆ **The Bridge to Terabithia**
By Paterson, Katherine

☆ **Where the Red Fern Grows**
By Rawls, Wilson

☆ **How to Eat Fried Worms**
By Rockwell, Thomas

☆ **Black Beauty**
By Sewell, Anna

☆ **Where the Sidewalk Ends**
By Silverstein, Shel

☆ **Encyclopedia Brown, Boy Detective**
By Sobol, Donald J

☆ **The Adventures of Tom Sawyer**
By Twain, Mark

☆ **Boxcar Children**
By Warner, Gertrude

☆ **Charlotte's Web**
By White, E.B.

☆ **Little House on the Prairie**
By Wilder, Laura

The key to a good summer reading list is having a wide variety of books that you enjoy! In addition to this list, visit the library to find more books. Ask the librarian for recommendations.

Skills Assessment Grade 3 - Math

1. Circle the number five thousand, two hundred fifteen.

    1,215   5,021   5,206   5,215

2. Write the numbers.

a. Four thousand, four hundred thirty-six =_____

b. Nine thousand, eight hundred twelve =_____

3. Write what number comes next. 1,997   1,998   1,999   _____

4. Write the numbers in order from smallest to largest.

134, 114, 411, 364. _____, _____, _____, _____.

5. In the number 2,876 there are:

_____ thousands _____ hundreds _____ tens and _____ ones.

6. Round to the nearest 10.

a. 146 = _____   b. 82 = _____   c. 648 = _____

7. Round to the nearest 100.

a. 560 = _____   b. 109 = _____   c. 795 = _____

8. Write 3,974 in expanded notation.

3,974=_____ + _____+_____+_____

9. Add or subtract to solve.

a. 482	b. 5,068	c. 6,284	d. 1,002
+ 67	+ 2,754	- 3,725	- 596

10. Multiply quickly.

7 x 2 = _____   5 x 1 = _____   4 x 2 = _____   7 x 3 = _____   6 x 2 = _____

3 x 3 = _____   9 x 2 = _____   5 x 7 = _____   8 x 4 = _____   3 x 8 = _____

6 x 3 = _____   7 x 8 = _____   5 x 9 = _____   8 x 7 = _____   6 x 8 = _____

2 x 11 = _____   6 x 9 = _____   6 x 6 = _____   3 x 9 = _____   4 x 4 = _____

9 x 4 = _____   5 x 3 = _____   8 x 8 = _____   7 x 6 = _____   3 x 4 = _____

11. Solve.

a. 326   b. 1,876   c. 6,786   d. 2,041
   x 4   x 5   x 9   x 8
  ____   _____   _____   _____

12. Divide. Work quickly.

a. $45 \div 9 =$ _____   c. $42 \div 7 =$ _____   e. $36 \div 6 =$ _____   g. $50 \div 5 =$ _____

b. $16 \div 4 =$ _____   d. $18 \div 3 =$ _____   f. $72 \div 8 =$ _____   h. $54 \div 9 =$ _____

13. Divide.

a. $5\overline{)77}$ b. $5\overline{)305}$ c. $4\overline{)3844}$ d. $4\overline{)1388}$

14. Color in parts to show each fraction.

a. 1/2   b. 1/4   c. 1/3   d. 2/4

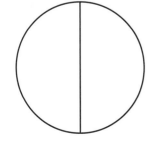
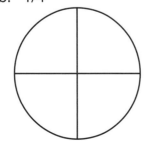

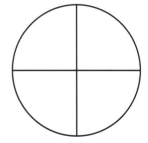

15. Circle the adjectives.

The small, gray mouse skittered across the tile floor and into its tiny hole.

16. Fill in the correct punctuation in each sentence.

a. Ouch that hurt

b. What time does the movie start

c. I am so happy to be on summer vacation

17. Write a synonym for each word. Ex. Glad= happy

a. scared = _____ b. wise = _____ c. finish = _____

18. Write an antonym for each word. Ex. In= out

a. above = _____ b. dark = _____ c. cold = _____

19 Circle the letters that should be capitalized in this sentence.

My aunt megan lives in seattle, washington.

20. Add commas where needed.

John Joseph and Gabe went camping in the mountains.

21. Write these words in alphabetical order.

freedom   factory   giant   harbor   group

_____, _____, _____, _____, _____.

22. Circle the correct homophone.

a. Sam got a new (pair, pear) of shoes for his birthday.

b. I (read, red) the book I got from the library all afternoon.

23. Write the contraction for each set of words.

a. I will = _____   b. you are = _____   c. it is = _____

24. Make each singular word plural.

a. wolf = _____   b. baby = _____   c. girl = _____

25. Add the correct suffix –ful, -est, -ing, -er.

a. Paulo is tall _____ than his brother Chad.

b. Sam is the tall_____ boy on the basketball team.

c. I like sing_____ in the shower.

Read the paragraph and answer the questions.

Neil Armstrong was an astronaut. In 1969, he did something nobody had done before when he walked on the moon. When he first stepped on the moon, he said, "One small step for man, one giant leap for mankind."

26. Circle the main idea of this paragraph.

a. The Phases of the moon   b. Rockets.   c. Who first walked on the moon.

27. Circle the correct way to break astronaut into syllables.

as-tr-o-naut   a-str-o-naut   as-tro-naut   astr-o-naut

28. Write four words that rhyme with moon.

_____, _____, _____, _____.

29. Circle the correct choice.

a. I (am , are) going to the beach today.

b. What (does, do) the word complicate mean?

c. I saw (a, an) elephant at the zoo.

d. Please water the plants over (their, there).

PARENT TIPS FOR WEEK 1

Skills of the Week

Weekly Value Honesty

- ✔ Idioms
- ✔ Rounding numbers
- ✔ Spiders
- ✔ Prime and composite numbers
- ✔ Synonyms
- ✔ Angles
- ✔ Adjectives
- ✔ Multiplication

Honesty means being fair, truthful, and trustworthy. Honesty means telling the truth no matter what. People who are honest do not lie, cheat, or steal.

Abraham Lincoln

Sometimes it is not easy to tell the truth, especially when you are scared and do not want to get in trouble or let others down. Try to remember that even when it is difficult telling the truth is always the best way to handle any situation and people will respect you more.

Play 60 Every Day!
Run, jump, dance and have fun outside every day for 60 minutes!

GET FIT TIME!

Weekly Extension Activities at SummerFitLearning.com

Honesty In Action!
Color the star each day you show honesty through your own actions.

WEEK 1

HEALTHY MIND + HEALTHY BODY

Color the ⭐ As You Complete Your Daily Task

	Day 1	Day 2	Day 3	Day 4	Day 5
MIND	⭐	⭐	⭐	⭐	⭐
BODY	⭐	⭐	⭐	⭐	⭐
DAILY READING	⭐ 20 minutes	⭐ 20 minutes	⭐ 20 minutes	⭐ 20 minutes	⭐ 20 minutes

You can do it!

"I am honest"

_____
Print Name

Idioms

Idioms are words, phrases, or expressions that cannot be taken literally. They have a second meaning. For example, "Once in a blue moon" means not very often.

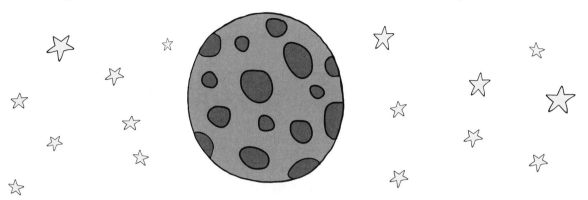

Read each sentence and circle the correct meaning of the idiom shown in quotations.

1.	Mom lets me stay up past midnight "once in a blue moon."
all the time	**Ex:** (not very often)
2.	After losing the tennis match, Mariah was "down in the dumps."
in the garbage	feeling bad
3.	My Grandpa "gets a kick out of" playing video games with me.
enjoys it	got kicked out
4.	Gabe told me I had won the contest but he was just "pulling my leg."
grabbing my foot	teasing me
5.	Dad couldn't "make heads or tails" out of the directions for the camera.
see the picture	understand
6.	Maddie was "playing with fire" when she was pulling the dog's tail.
taking a risk	playing with matches

Draw a line to match the idiom with the meaning.

7. Raining cats and dogs	Go to bed
8. Ants in your pants	Go ahead and eat
9. Hit the hay	Pouring rain
10. Your head is in the clouds	Easy
11. Chow down	Don't know what to say
12. Cat's got your tongue	Wiggling around
13. Piece of cake	Day dreaming

Aerobic

DAILY EXERCISE
Jogging for Fitness 5
"Stretch Before You Play!"

Instruction
Jog 5 minutes in place or outside

Be Healthy!
Breakfast is the most important meal of the day!

DAY 1

2

3

4

5

WEEK 1

Rounding Off

Rounding a number means you "bump" it up or down to a nearby number. The rules of rounding are simple.

If the number you are rounding is followed by a 5,6,7,8,or 9, round the number up. Ex: 38 = 40	If the number you are rounding is followed by a 0,1,2,3,or 4, round the number down. Ex: 34 = 30

Round to the nearest ten	Round to the nearest hundred
58 = 60	345 = 300
145 = 150	887 = 900

1. 63 = _____

2. 168 = _____

3. 292 = _____

4. 359 = _____

5. 98 = _____

6. 387 = _____

7. 127 = _____

8. 765 = _____

9. 126 = _____

10. 156 = _____

11. 623 = _____

12. 3,975 = _____

13. 5,230 = _____

14. 8,432 = _____

Round to the nearest thousand.

15. 2,345 = _____

16. 7,620 = _____

17. 4,922 = _____

18. 1,120 = _____

19. 1,987 = _____

20. 5,450 = _____

21. 6,834 = _____

22. 9,876 = _____

23. 8,320 = _____

- Arachnophobia is the fear of spiders and is one of the most common fears of humans.
- Are you afraid of spiders? Learning about something can help you overcome your fears.
- Spiders have 48 knees.
- Tarantulas can live up to 30 years!

Read the passage on spiders and answer the questions below.

A spider is an arachnid. Arachnids have four pairs of jointed legs and two distinct body parts, the head and abdomen.   There are more than 30,000 species of spiders. Spiders come in all shapes, sizes, and colors, and while they may seem scary, most spiders are not harmful to humans. All spiders have eight legs, and as many as eight eyes.   Spiders don't have ears but "hear" by feeling sound vibrations with the tiny hairs that cover their legs.

As spiders grow, they molt and leave their old tight skin behind when they grow a new one. Spiders can molt many times during their lifetime. Spiders live in hot and cold climates and live on every continent except Antarctica. Spiders can be found in many different places: houses, gardens, underground, and even in water. Not all spiders spin webs, but the ones that do spin silk thread from their spinnerets. Some spiders are poisonous, such as the black widow and the brown recluse, but most are harmless and spend their days eating insects, which would otherwise take over the planet!

1. A spider is an _____.

2. Describe the characteristic of a spider. _____.

3. How do spiders "hear"? _____

4. What is it called when spiders shed their own skin? _____

5. A spider spins a web with its _____.

6. A spider's two main body parts are the _____ and the _____.

Strength
Go to www.summerfitlearning.com for more Activities!

DAILY EXERCISE
Knee lifts
"Stretch Before You Play!"

Instruction
Repeat 5 times with each leg

Be Healthy!
Help set the table for dinner today!

DAY 2

1
3
4
5

WEEK 1

Prime Numbers

A prime number is a whole number greater than 1 that has exactly two factors, 1 and itself. A composite number is a whole number that is greater than 1 and has more than two factors. The number 1 is a special case and is neither prime nor composite.

Circle all the prime numbers between 1 and 50. Hint: there are 15. Put a square around the number that is neither prime nor composite.

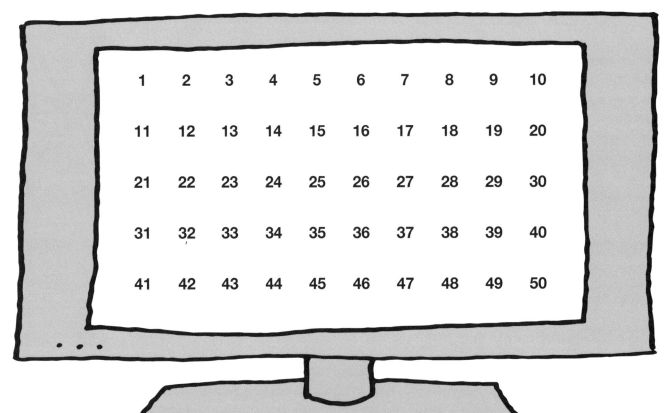

1	2	3	4	5	6	7	8	9	10
11	12	13	14	15	16	17	18	19	20
21	22	23	24	25	26	27	28	29	30
31	32	33	34	35	36	37	38	39	40
41	42	43	44	45	46	47	48	49	50

List 5 composite numbers between 1 and 50.

_____, _____, _____, _____, _____,

Synonyms are words that have the same meaning as another word. Antonyms are words that have the opposite meaning.

Draw a line to match each word with its antonym.

Ex:
1. wet	loud
2. awake	go
3. happy	float
4. stop	dry
5. sink	white
6. black	sad
7. quiet	asleep

1
2
DAY
3
4
5

Write a synonym to replace each underlined word.

8. I sat on the <u>sofa</u> and read my book._____

9. Mom found a <u>giant</u> spider in the garden. _____

10. Albert Einstein was very <u>intelligent</u>. _____

11. I rode the roller coaster at the <u>carnival</u>. _____

12. Mr. Brown was <u>glad</u> when he found his lost dog, Spot._____

13. When I saw George up ahead, I <u>shouted</u> to get his attention. _____

W E E K 1

Aerobic

Go to www.summerfitlearning.com for more Activities!

DAILY EXERCISE
Jumping Jacks
"Stretch Before You Play!"

Instruction
20 Jumping Jacks

Be Healthy!
Ask your parents about what foods are good for you.

Angles

Right Angle.	Obtuse Angle	Acute Angle
A right angle is a 90 degree angle and makes an L shape.	An obtuse angle is greater than 90 degrees.	An acute angle is a "cute little" angle that is less than 90 degrees.

Label each angle. Use 1 for right angles, 2 for obtuse angels and 3 for acute angles.

1. _____

2. _____

3. _____

4. _____

5. _____

6. _____

7. _____

8. _____

9. _____

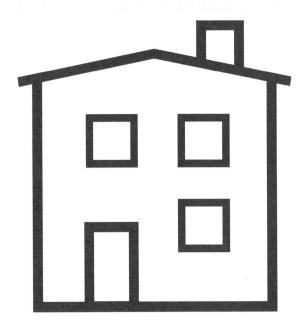

Circle all the angles in the picture.

10. How many right angles?_____

11. How many obtuse angles? _____

12. How many acute angles?_____

Amazing Adjectives

Adjectives are descriptive words. Adjectives are used to describe or modify another person or thing in the sentence. Choose adjectives from the list to answer the questions.

ADJECTIVES				
honest	slimy	trustworthy	smelly	fast
pretty	creative	loving	beautiful	busy
lazy	hot	funny	clever	fuzzy
strong	kind	noisy	windy	colorful
sweet	juicy	rotten	studious	delicious

1. Choose 3 adjectives to describe your mother.

_____, _____, _____

2. What 2 adjectives describe a bag of garbage?

_____, _____

3. Choose 3 adjectives to describe what kind of student you are.

_____, _____, _____

4. Describe a summer day.

_____, _____, _____

5. What adjectives describe your best friend?

_____, _____, _____

6. Describe strawberries.

_____, _____, _____

Circle the adjectives in the following sentences.

7. Mom made a delicious dinner and chocolate cake for my 8th birthday.

8. The soft, furry hamster burrowed into his tiny nest.

9. I am wearing a striped shirt and my new, blue jeans to the circus.

Strength

Go to www.summerfitlearning.com for more Activities!

DAILY EXERCISE
Chin-ups
"Stretch Before You Play!"

Instruction
Repeat 2 times

Be Healthy!
Talk about your day with your family.

1   **2**   **3**   **DAY 4**   **5**

WEEK 1

Times Tables

Use the grid to fill in your time tables.

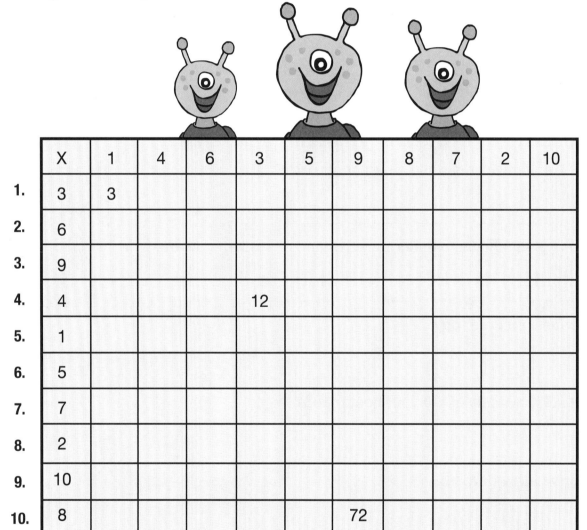

	X	1	4	6	3	5	9	8	7	2	10
1.	3	3									
2.	6										
3.	9										
4.	4				12						
5.	1										
6.	5										
7.	7										
8.	2										
9.	10										
10.	8						72				

Use your completed times table to solve these problems.

11. (10 x 10) + (6 x 5) + (2 x 4) = _____

12. (7 x 7) + (3 x 1) - (5 x 2) = _____

Honesty means being fair, truthful, and trustworthy. Honesty means telling the truth no matter what. People who are honest do not lie, cheat, or steal.

Honest Abe

Abraham Lincoln was an honest man. He worked hard all his life and believed that being honest was very important. Lincoln was born in a log cabin on February 12, 1809. When he was only 9 years old, his mother died. Lincoln had to work hard to help his father so he wasn't able to go to school much. Instead he read books. Lincoln loved to read and learned a lot.

Lincoln became the 16th president of the United States of America. During his presidency he helped end slavery and kept the states together.

Use the words to fill in the blanks.

| slavery | log cabin | read | honesty | president |

1. Abraham Lincoln was born in a _____.

2. He loved to _____ books.

3. Abraham was known for his _____.

4. Abraham Lincoln was the 16th _____ of the United States of America.

5. When he was president he helped end _____.

Choose 1 or more activities to do with your family or friends. Color today's star when you are finished. Good job!

☐ Write down as many examples of how people cheat (on tests, at sports etc.).

☐ Create a bookmark on honesty. Think about "Honest Abe" when you use it to mark your place.

Core Value Book List
Read More About Honesty

Liar, Liar Pants on Fire
By Diane DeGroat

Summer Wheels
By Eve Bunting

Lizzie Lies A lot
By Elizabeth Levy

Reading Extension
Activities at
SummerFitLearning.com

☐ Think about the quote "Oh what a tangled web we weave, when first we practice to deceive." Gather your friends and family and some yarn. Spread out around the room and tell everyone to answer the question dishonestly. Ask questions like "Did you eat the cookie?" As each person answers, have them wrap the end of the yarn around some part of their body before passing it to the next person. The point is to show that one lie often leads to another and how easy it is to get trapped and embarrassed by our lies.

Let's Talk About It

Discuss with your child how they can demonstrate honesty in different situations: cashier gives too much change, friend asks to copy answers for homework, find $5.00 at the library, promised mom you would clean your room but played video games instead. Talk about the consequences of being dishonest like losing the respect of others, being embarrassed when caught in a lie, having to tell more lies, and feeling bad. Remind them that telling the truth and being honest is the right thing to do.

Play Time!
Choose a Game or Activity to Play for 60 minutes today!

YOU CHOOSE

Write down which game or activity you played today!

Be Healthy!
Wash your hands before every meal.

1 2 3 4

DAY 5

WEEK 1

WEEK 2

PARENT TIPS FOR WEEK 2

Skills of the Week

✔ Plurals
✔ Congruent shapes
✔ Helping verbs
✔ Possessive pronouns
✔ Roman numerals
✔ Prefixes
✔ Expanded and word form
✔ Animal riddles
✔ Fractions.

Weekly Value Compassion

Mother Teresa

Compassion is caring about the feelings and needs of others.

Sometimes we are so focused on our own feelings that we don't care how other people feel. If we consider other's feelings before our own the world can be a much kinder place. Take time to do something nice for another person and you will feel better about yourself.

GET FIT TIME!

Play 60 Every Day!

Run, jump, dance and have fun outside every day for 60 minutes!

Weekly Extension Activities at SummerFitLearning.com

Compassion In Action!

Color the star each day you show compassion through your own actions.

29

WEEK 2

Color the ⭐ As You Complete Your Daily Task

	Day 1	Day 2	Day 3	Day 4	Day 5
MIND	⭐	⭐	⭐	⭐	⭐
BODY	⭐	⭐	⭐	⭐	⭐
DAILY READING	⭐	⭐	⭐	⭐	⭐
	20 minutes	20 minutes	20 minutes	20 minutes	20 minutes

You can do it!

"I am compassionate"

_____
Print Name

A plural form of a word is needed when a word is used to describe more than one. Rewrite each word in its plural form.

Ex: peach	peaches
1. goose	
2. mouse	
3. box	
4. boy	
5. dog	
6. baby	
7. man	
8. puppy	
9. table	
10. calf	

11. coat	
12. fish	
13. watch	
14. wolf	
15. leaf	
16. lady	
17. bunny	
18. monkey	
19. dish	
20. letter	

DAY 1

2

3

4

5

WEEK 2

Aerobic

Go to www.summerfitlearning.com for more Activities!

DAILY EXERCISE
Let's Jump
"Stretch Before You Play!"

Instruction
3 Sets of Jumps

Be Healthy!
Give your parents a hug.

DAY 1

WEEK 2

2 3 4 5

Congruency

Figures that are the same size and shape are congruent. Write yes or no if the shapes are congruent.

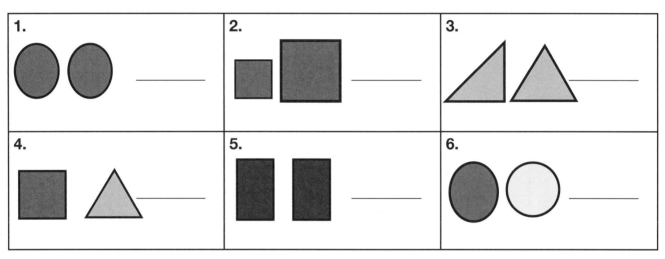

1. _____

2. _____

3. _____

4. _____

5. _____

6. _____

Circle the shapes that are congruent in each row.

7.

8.

9.

© Summer Fit

am	is	will	are	were	was

Fill in the blank with a helping verb from the box.

1. My friends and I _____ have a picnic in the park tomorrow.

2. Today I _____ going swimming with my Aunt Megan.

3. We _____ fishing at the lake yesterday when it began to rain.

4. Tomorrow we _____ going to the carnival.

5. The baby _____ sleeping now so we must play quietly.

6. I _____ riding my bike when I hit a rock and fell.

Possessive Pronouns

Some pronouns are used to show possession or ownership. Choose the possessive pronouns that best complete the sentence and write them on the line.

7. _____ mom planted flowers in the yard. (My/Mine) Gardening is _____ favorite hobby. (her/hers)

8. Grace finished _____ art project (her/hers) but Maddie will finish _____ tomorrow. (her/hers)

9. _____ family enjoys fishing and camping together. (Our/Ours)

10. Please remember to clean _____ room before you go outside to play. (your, yours)

11. Mr. and Mrs. Star painted _____ house. (their, theirs)

12. _____ sister was in a play last night. (My/Mine) It was _____ first time in a leading role. (her/hers)

13. Dad trimmed the apple tree in _____ yard (our/ours) because _____ branches were overgrown. (its/your)

14. My brother fell off _____ bike (his/hers) and broke _____ arm (his/hers).

15. Sally likes to wear _____ hair down (her/hers) but Judith likes to wear _____ in pony tails. (her/hers)

16. This cookie is _____ (my/mine) and that cookie is _____ (your/yours).

Strength
Go to www.summerfitlearning.com for more Activities!

DAILY EXERCISE
Bottle curls
"Stretch Before You Play!"

Instruction
Repeat 5 times
with each arm

Be Healthy!
Shop for food
with your
parents.

1

DAY **2**

3

4

5

W E E K 2

Roman Numerals

Roman numerals come from the numeral system of ancient Rome. It is based on some of the letters of the alphabet that can be combined to represent numbers that are the sum of their values.

I = 1	V = 5	X = 10	L=50	C=100

Draw a line from the Arabic numeral to the correct Roman numeral.

1. 6	VIII
2. 8	II
3. 2	IV
4. 4	VI

5. 10	XIII
6. 5	IX
7. 13	X
8. 9	V

9. Write the Arabic numeral for each Roman numeral.

XX _____	XVII _____	XIX _____
XXVII _____	C _____	IV _____
LXII _____	XL _____	XXIII _____

10. Write the Roman numeral for each Arabic numeral.

36 _____	55 _____	14 _____
29 _____	40 _____	21 _____

11. Fill in the missing Roman numerals.

I _____, III, _____, _____, VI, _____, _____, _____, X, _____, _____.

The prefix **re** usually means do again. Rewrap means wrap again.	The prefix **de** usually means from, down, or away. Depart means go away from.
The prefix **pre** usually means before. Preview means view before.	The prefix **ex** usually means out of or from. Export means send out of.

Read each word, circle the prefix and write the root word on the line. Then write what the word means.

1. (re)wash **Ex.** _____wash_____ _____wash again_____

2. exchange _____ _____

3. rebuild _____ _____

4. decrease _____ _____

5. reteach _____ _____

6. detour _____ _____

7. preschool _____ _____

8. redo _____ _____

9. prepay _____ _____

10. exclaim _____ _____

Choose three words from the list above and put them into sentences.

11. _____

_____

12. _____

_____

13. _____

_____

Aerobic Go to www.summerfitlearning.com for more Activities!

DAILY EXERCISE
Let's Dance
"Stretch Before You Play!"

Instruction
Dance for 5 Minutes

Be Healthy!
Write down 3 healthy foods you like.

Expanded and Word Form

Write the following in standard form

1. Nine hundred twenty-five = _____

2. Seven thousand four hundred sixteen = _____

3. Three hundred seventy-five = _____

4. Two hundred fourteen = _____

Write in words

5. 320 = _____

6. 1,852 = _____

7. 5,248 = _____

8. 3,980 = _____

Write in expanded form	Write the number
9. Ex. 598 = 500 + 90 + 8	13. 1,000 + 700 + 40 + 3 = _____
10. 4,367 = _____	14. 3,000 + 500 + 20 + 9 = _____
11. 6,781 = _____	15. 9,000 + 200 + 60 + 5 = _____
12. 8,103 = _____	16. 5,000 + 900 + 80 + 2 = _____

Write the number that is halfway between.

17. Ex. 200, 400 = 300	19. 60, 70 = _____	21. 75, 95 = _____
18. 500, 700 = _____	20. 6,000, 8,000 = _____	22. 150, 250 = _____

Match each description with the correct animal in the sentences below.

capybara	**woodpecker**
hummingbird	**chameleon**
penguin	**raccoon**

1. My wings beat at 80-100 strokes per second. I get all my energy from the sugar in the nectar I drink. I am a _____.

2. I live among the trees and hammer into their trunks with my sharp bill to find insect larvae, sap, or to build a nest hole. I am a _____.

3. I am slow moving and rely on my ability to change color to protect myself. I live in a tree and use my flexible tail to cling to branches while I trap insects with my long, sticky tongue. I am a _____.

4. Even though I am a bird I cannot fly. My feet are powerful flippers and help me swim fast in the cold Antarctic Ocean. I am a _____.

5. I am the world's largest rodent and am the size of a sheep. I look like my relative the guinea pig and live in South America. I am a _____.

6. I live in North America and am easily recognized by my striped tail and black circles around my eyes. I like to raid garbage cans to look for food and am usually nocturnal. I am a_____ _____.

Stretch your brain.....

Name the two continents mentioned in the sentences above.

_____ , _____

Divide these words into syllables.

hummingbird   _____   _____   _____

woodpecker   _____   _____   _____

capybara   _____   _____   _____   _____

---

1 2 3 DAY 4 5

WEEK 2

DAILY EXERCISE
Heel Raises
"Stretch Before You Play!"

Instruction
Repeat 8 times

Be Healthy!
Use sunscreen when you play outside!

Fractions

Parts of a whole.

How many parts are shaded?   2   How many parts in all?   3

The shaded part is   2/3   The unshaded part is   1/3

Write the fraction that shows the shaded part in the different shapes.

1.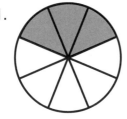

2.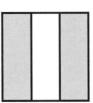

3.

Ex: 3/8 _____

_____

_____

4.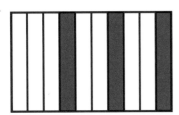

5.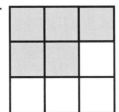

6.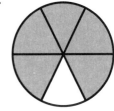

_____

_____

_____

Write <, >, or = for the fractions below.

7. 1/2 circle _____ 2/4 circle   8. 1/4 square _____ 3/4 square

Shade the fraction of each shape.

9.   **3/5**   10.   **2/3**   11.   **7/10**

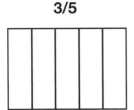

Compassion is caring about the feelings and needs of others.

Mother Teresa

As a young woman Mother Teresa decided she wanted to be a missionary in order to spread love and compassion in the world. Mother Teresa spent her life taking care of people in India who had nobody to take care of them including the poor, orphaned and sick. She took care of thousands of people who were unwanted and unloved and she did it without asking for anything in return. Mother Teresa showed compassion because she always put the interest of others in front of her own. Even when she was suffering from illness, she continued to care for others and never gave up on her goal of helping all those in need.

Write three examples of how someone has shown compassion to you.

1. _____

2. _____

3. _____

Write three examples of how you have shown compassion to others.

4. _____

5. _____

6. _____

Choose 1 or more activities to do with your family or friends. Color today's star when you are finished. Good job!

☐ You can make a difference in your community and your world. Collect food from your family, friends, and neighbors. Make cards for or collect stuffed animals for kids in the hospital suffering from cancer.

☐ Organize a neighborhood clean up. Pick up garbage, pull weeds, plant flowers. Offer to do yard work for elderly neighbors or neighbors who could use a hand.

☐ Think of 3 ways you can be a hero of compassion in your daily life. Now practice them.

Core Value Book List
Read More About Compassion

The Hundred Penny Box
By Sharon Bell Mathis

The Selfish Giant
By Oscar Wilde

The Family Under the Bridge
By Natalie Savage Carlson

Reading Extension Activities at SummerFitLearning.com

Let's Talk About It

Talk with your child about compassionate people in the world. Help your child discover his or her gifts and think of ways they can use them to help others. As always, you are your child's best teacher. Children learn what they live. Provide them with different opportunities to volunteer and serve others.

Stepping Stones

Stepping Stones Entertainment™ was founded by parents who wanted to provide meaningful family movies to help inspire common values. It is made up of people from many different backgrounds, nationalities and beliefs. For more than 20 years, Stepping Stones has provided families with movies about integrity, charity, forgiveness and many other common values through hundreds of films for all ages. Learn more at **www.steppingstones.com**.

STEPPING STONES.com
Meaningful Family Movies

Play Time!
Choose a Game or Activity to Play for 60 minutes today!

YOU CHOOSE

Write down which game or activity you played today!

Be Healthy! Plant a vegetable garden.

DAY 5

WEEK 3

PARENT TIPS FOR WEEK 3

Skills of the Week

✔ Poetry
✔ Multiplication
✔ Common and proper nouns
✔ Addition and subtraction
✔ Patterns
✔ Past, present and future nouns
✔ Adding 3 numbers
✔ Making a ten
✔ Sequencing numbers
✔ Time
✔ Homophones
✔ Perimeter

Weekly Value Trustworthiness

Harriet Tubman

Trustworthiness is being worthy of trust. It means people can count on you.

You are honest and you keep your word. Sometimes it is easy to forget what we tell people because we try to do too much or we are constantly moving around. Try to slow down and follow through on what you say before moving onto something else.

GET FIT TIME!

Play 60 Every Day!

Run, jump, dance and have fun outside every day for 60 minutes!

Weekly Extension Activities at SummerFitLearning.com

Trust In Action!

Color the star each day you show trustworthiness through your own actions

41

WEEK 3

HEALTHY MIND + HEALTHY BODY

Color the ⭐ As You Complete Your Daily Task

	Day 1	Day 2	Day 3	Day 4	Day 5
MIND	⭐	⭐	⭐	⭐	⭐
BODY	⭐	⭐	⭐	⭐	⭐
DAILY READING	⭐ 20 minutes	⭐ 20 minutes	⭐ 20 minutes	⭐ 20 minutes	⭐ 20 minutes

You can do it!

"I am trustworthy"

_____
Print Name

Read the poem aloud and answer the questions below.

Where Go The Boats?
By Robert Louis Stevenson

Dark brown I the river,
Golden is the sand,
It flows along forever,
With trees on either hand.

Green leaves afloating,
Castles of the foam,
Boats of mine a - boating -
Where will all come home?

On goes the river,
And out past the mill,
Away down the valley,
Away down the hill.

Away down the river,
A hundred miles or more,
Other little children
Shall bring my boats ashore.

Robert Louis Stevenson

Extra Credit: Look up the poet Robert Louis Stevenson. Find out when he lived and where he was from. Read some of his other poems such as "Foreign Lands," "Bed in Summer," and - "My Bed is a Boat." Try to memorize the poem "Where go the Boats."

DAY
1

2

3

4

5

1. What do you think this poem is about? _____

2. What are the adjectives used to describe the river in the first stanza? _____

3. What are the plural words in the second stanza? _____, _____,

_____.

4. After reading the third stanza, are the boats in the poem going far away or not too far?

_____ .

5. What are the rhyming words in the last stanza? _____, _____.

6. Do you like this poem? _____ Why or why not? _____

_____

W E E K 3

Aerobic

Go to www.summerfitlearning.com for more Activities!

DAILY EXERCISE
Pass and Go
"Stretch Before You Play!"

Instruction
Get a Friend to Play
this Game With You!

Be Healthy!
Eat breakfast
with your
family.

DAY **1**

2

3

4

5

WEEK 3

Monster Math

Monster Multiplication Review. Multiply to find your answers.

1. 3 x 4 ____   3 x 5 ____   3 x 10 ____   3 x 9 ____   3 x 2 ____

   3 x 6 ____   3 x 8 ____   3 x 1 ____   3 x 7 ____   3 x 3 ____

2. 6 x 6 ____   6 x 2 ____   6 x 5 ____   6 x 4 ____   6 x 9 ____

   6 x 3 ____   6 x 7 ____   6 x 10 ____   6 x 8 ____   6 x 1 ____

3. 4 x 5 ____   4 x 3 ____   4 x 1 ____   4 x 10 ____   4 x 6 ____

   4 x 2 ____   4 x 7 ____   4 x 4 ____   4 x 9 ____   4 x 8 ____

4. 8 x 3 ____   8 x 10 ____   8 x 6 ____   8 x 8 ____   8 x 2 ____

   8 x 4 ____   8 x 1 ____   8 x 7 ____   8 x 9 ____   8 x 5 ____

5. 5 x 10 ____   5 x 1 ____   5 x 6 ____   5 x 2 ____   5 x 4 ____

   5 x 8 ____   5 x 7 ____   5 x 3 ____   5 x 9 ____   5 x 5 ____

6. 7 x 3 ____   7 x 2 ____   7 x 8 ____   7 x 9 ____   7 x 5 ____

   7 x 7 ____   7 x 4 ____   7 x 6 ____   7 x 1 ____   7 x 10 ____

44

© Summer Fit

A noun is a name of a person, place, or thing.
Write PERSON, PLACE, or THING beside each noun.

1. car _____   6. library _____   11. park _____

2. chair _____   7. fireman _____   12. teacher _____

3. bank _____   8. baby _____   13. brother _____

4. nurse _____   9. kitchen _____   14. moon _____

5. mouse _____   10. book _____   15. restaurant _____

A proper noun is a specific person, place, or thing. Proper nouns always begin with a capital letter.

Write a common noun for each proper noun.

16. Toy Story = movie   20. Bob's Pet Store _____

17. September _____   21. Maple Avenue _____

18. Arizona _____   22. Poodle _____

19. Christmas _____   23. James _____

Write a proper noun for each common noun.

24. weekday _____   28. girl _____

25. state _____   29. month _____

26. store _____   30. country _____

27. teacher _____   31. school _____

Strength

Go to www.summerfitlearning.com for more Activities!

DAILY EXERCISE
Squats
"Stretch Before You Play!"

Instruction
Repeat 6 Times

Be Healthy! Drink small amounts of water while playing.

Mixed Practice

Mixed practice. Add and subtract to find your answers.

1. 289 − 146	**3.** 334 + 215	**5.** 678 - 427	**7.** 521 - 310
2. 430 + 268	**4.** 765 - 231	**6.** 978 − 426	**8.** 152 + 137

Fill in the missing number to complete the equation.

Ex: 6 x __5__ = 30	**9.** _____ x 9 = 18	**10.** 5 x 8 =_____	**11.** 3 x _____= 21
12. 6 x 8 = _____	**13.** 7 x _____ = 35	**14.** 2 x _____ = 20	**15.** _____ x 6= 24
16. 4 x 9 = _____	**17.** 9 x _____ = 27	**18.** _____ x 5 = 20	**19.** 4 x 4 = _____

Finish the counting patterns.

20. 50, 45, _____, _____, _____, _____, _____, _____, _____, _____, 0

21. 20, 22, 24, _____, _____, _____, _____, _____, _____, _____, _____

22. 12, 15, _____, _____, _____, _____, _____, _____, _____, _____

23. 130, 140, _____, _____, _____, _____, _____, _____, _____, _____

DAY **2**

WEEK 3

1 3 4 5

© Summer Fit

Nouns and Verbs

Trustworthiness

Nouns are words that name a person, place, or thing. Verbs are action words. Circle the verbs and underline the nouns.

1.

run	cloud	swim	dog	eat	jump
fence	boy	hop	sing	apple	drink
whisper	house	spider	crawl	tree	bark

Verbs can tell what is happening now (present), what happened yesterday (past), and what will happen tomorrow (future). Use the correct verb to complete each sentence.

2. Swim, swam, will swim. We like to _____.

   We _____ yesterday.

   We _____ at the lake next week.

3. Play, played, will play   I _____ baseball every day with my friends.

   I _____ baseball with my dad last Saturday.

   I _____ baseball with my uncle tomorrow.

4. Sing, sang, will sing   I like to _____ in the shower.

   I _____ to the baby last night.

   I _____ in the choir on Sunday.

5. Draw, drew, will draw   The artist likes to _____ kids at the zoo.

   Sam _____ a picture for the art show next week.

   I _ _____ a picture for my grandma tomorrow

1

2

DAY 3

4

5

WEEK 3

Aerobic

Go to www.summerfitlearning.com for more Activities!

DAILY EXERCISE
Step It Up
"Stretch Before You Play!"

Instruction
Start Slow &
Increase Your Speed

Be Healthy!
Eat different types to get all the nutrients you need!

1
2
DAY 3
4
5

WEEK 3

Adding Multiple Numbers

1.	64	2.	52	3.	76	4.	39
	34		30		24		16
	+ 22		+ 15		+ 48		+ 25

Add.

5. 5 + 6 + 4 + 9 = _____

6. 9 + 3 + 1 +7 = _____

7. 5 + 1 + 4 + 2 = _____

8. 6 + 4 + 7 + 3 = _____

9. 8 + 5 + 2 + 7 = _____

10. 8 + 5 + 2 + 4 = _____

Write the numbers that come before, between, or after.

11. 49, _____, 51

12. 99, _____, 101

13. _____, 300, _____

14. _____, 19, 20

15. 348, _____, 350

16. 1, 276, _____

17. _____, 5,000, _____

18. 8,999, _____

19. 999, _____, 1,001

What time is it?

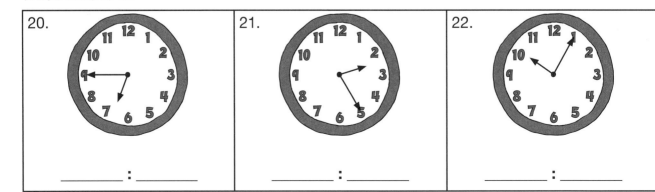

20. _____ : _____

21. _____ : _____

22. _____ : _____

Homophones are words that sound the same but have different meanings and spellings. Choose the correct homophone for each sentence. Circle it and write it on the line.

1. The dog wagged its _____ when I gave him a bone.   (tale, tail)

2. My brother's birthday is next _____.   (week, weak)

3. I ate _____ much candy, and now I feel sick.   (to, two, too)

4. I _____ two library books yesterday.   (read, red)

5. Do you _____ your times tables?   (no, know)

6. It is important to _____ thank you notes.   (right, write)

7. _____ do you go camping?   (Wear, Where)

8. The recipe calls for 2 cups of _____ and 1 cup of sugar.   (flower, flour)

9. My library books are _____ on Thursday.   (dew, due)

10. There was snow on the mountain _____.   (peak, peek)

11. A _____ chicken is called a rooster, while a female is a hen.   (mail, male)

12. There was a _____ under the sink, so my mom called the plumber.   (leek, leak)

Strength
Go to www.summerfitlearning.com for more Activities!

DAILY EXERCISE
Lunges
"Stretch Before You Play!"

Instruction
Repeat 5 times
with each leg

Be Healthy!
Drinking milk
builds strong
bones and
teeth!

Perimeter

A perimeter is the total distance around a shape.   Write the perimeter of each shape.

1.
6 cm
2 cm

_____

2.
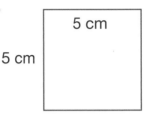
5 cm
5 cm

_____

3.

7 cm
4 cm

_____

4.

9 cm
9 cm

_____

5.

12 cm
5 cm

_____

6.
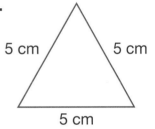
5 cm   5 cm
5 cm

_____

7.
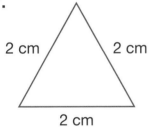
2 cm   2 cm
2 cm

_____

8.
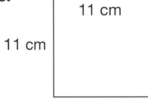
11 cm
11 cm

_____

9.
20 cm
6 cm

_____

10. Use a ruler to draw a square with a perimeter of 8 cm.

50 © Summer Fit

WEEK 3

1
2
3
DAY
4
5

Trustworthiness is being worthy of trust. It means people can count on you. You are honest and you keep your word.

Harriet Tubman was a slave before the Civil War. Being a slave meant that she had no property, no rights, and had to do whatever her master told her. Harriet had to work hard but even as a little girl she dreamed of being free. Although she was small, Harriet was strong and even more strong-willed. When she was an adult, Harriet escaped to the North where she was free. Being free herself wasn't enough for Harriet. She wanted other slaves to be free as well. Harriet led hundreds of slaves to freedom using the "Underground Railroad" which was a secret system of hiding places to help slaves escape. At one time there was a $40,000 reward offered by slave owners for her capture. Each time she went back to help more slaves, she risked her life. People trusted Harriet with their lives and she never let them down.

Being trustworthy is difficult because it includes having to display several characteristics including; HONESTY, COURAGE, FRIENDSHIP AND being RELIABLE.

Below, write a short sentence next to each word telling how Harriet Tubman displayed each of these characteristics.

1. Honesty (does not lie cheat or steal): _____

2. Courage (do what is right even when it is difficult): _____

3. Friendship (do not betray someone's trust): _____

4. Reliable (keep promises and follow through on commitment): _____

5. Which of these qualities is your strongest? _____

6. Which of these qualities is your weakest? _____

Choose 1 or more activities to do with your family or friends. Color today's star when you are finished. Good job!

☐ Think of symbols to represent trustworthiness. Make a shield or family crest that represents your trustworthiness using your symbols.

☐ Learn about seeing-eye dogs. The sight-impaired people who use them have complete trust in them.

☐ Learn more about the "Underground Railroad" and about the trust needed to make that risky journey to freedom. What happened to the slaves who were caught? What happened to the people who were helping them? Share what you have learned with your family or friends.

☐ Write a song or poem about trustworthiness.

Core Value Book List
Read More About Trustworthiness

Courage of Sarah Noble
By Alice Dalgliesh

Twenty and Ten
By Puffin Book

After the Goat Man
By Betsy Byars

Reading Extension
Activities at
SummerFitLearning.com

Let's Talk About It

Kids this age start relying more on their friends for support and approval. Talk about the qualities that make up a good friend. What makes a friend trustworthy? Talk about the trust you have that they will make good choices when they are with their friends. Role play different situations they may find themselves in.

Play Time!

Choose a Game or Activity to Play for 60 minutes today!

YOU CHOOSE

_____

Write down which game or activity you played today!

Be Healthy!
Ask your parents to teach you more about eating healthy!

WEEK 3

DAY 5

1

2

3

4

PARENT TIPS FOR WEEK 4

Skills of the Week

✔ Analogies
✔ Money math
✔ Suffixes, prefixes, and root words
✔ Place value
✔ The human skeleton
✔ Time
✔ Antonyms
✔ Fast facts
✔ Adding a 10
✔ Adding a 100

Weekly Value Self-Discipline

Stephanie Lopez Cox

Self-discipline means self-control. It is working hard and getting yourself to do what is important.

It is easy to lose interest in what you are doing, especially if it does not come fast and easy. Focus your attention on what you are trying to accomplish and try to block out other things until you reach your goal.

GET FIT TIME!

Play 60 Every Day!
Run, jump, dance and have fun outside every day for 60 minutes!

Weekly Extension Activities at SummerFitLearning.com

Self-Discipline In Action!
Color the star each day you show self-discipline through your own actions.

WEEK 4

HEALTHY MIND + HEALTHY BODY

Color the ⭐ As You Complete Your Daily Task

	Day 1	Day 2	Day 3	Day 4	Day 5
MIND	⭐	⭐	⭐	⭐	⭐
BODY	⭐	⭐	⭐	⭐	⭐
DAILY READING	⭐ 20 minutes	⭐ 20 minutes	⭐ 20 minutes	⭐ 20 minutes	⭐ 20 minutes

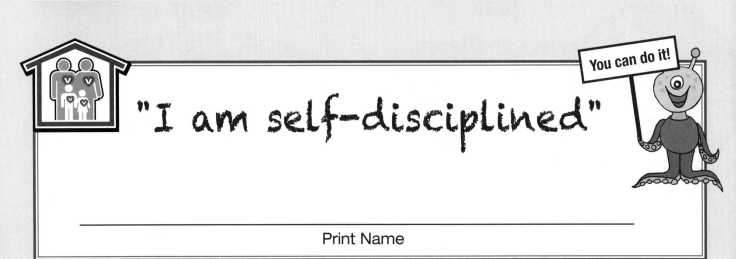

You can do it!

"I am self-disciplined"

_____
Print Name

An analogy is a comparison of similarities. Fill in the missing words to complete the analogies. ⊡ = "is to" and ⊡⊡ = "as".

> **Example: Puppy : dog :: cat : kitten = Puppy is to dog as cat is to kitten.**

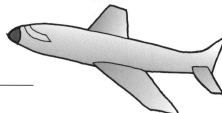

1. up : down :: in : _____

2. airplane : air :: ship : _____

3. boy : man :: girl : _____

4. wolf : pack :: fish : _____

5. smile : happy :: frown : _____

6. apple : fruit :: broccoli : _____

7. sun : day :: moon : _____

8. hand : arm :: foot : _____

9. eye : see :: ear : _____

10 fire : hot :: ice : _____

11. write : letter :: read : _____

12. calf : cow :: lamb : _____

DAILY EXERCISE
Kangaroo Bounce
"Stretch Before You Play!"

Instruction
Jump 10 Times

Be Healthy!
A calorie is a unit of energy.

DAY 1

2

3

4

5

`1+2=3` `+` `-` `=` `×` `÷`

Money Matters

Count the money and write the amount. Remember your dollar sign ($) and decimal point (.).

1.	
2.	
3.	
4.	

Answer the story problems by writing the amount.

5. I have 2 quarters and 3 nickels less than $1.00. _____

6. I have 3 quarters and 2 dimes more than $5.00. _____

7. Draw a picture to show $3.62.

Make dollars and cents then read each amount.

8.

Ex. 89 __$ .89__   125 _____   670 _____   1050 _____   1500 _____

5975 _____   2550 _____   09 _____   1246 _____   10065 _____

Root Word	**Prefix**	**Suffix**
A root word is a word you can make into a new word by adding a beginning or an ending.	A prefix is a word part added to the beginning of a root word to create a word with a different meaning.	A suffix is a word part added to the end of a root word to create a word with a different meaning.

Prefix & Suffix: beginnings & endings

un = not	ful = full of	less = without
re = again	er = one who	dis = not

Read each root word and add the suffix. Write the new word on the line.

1. pay + ment = payment

2. wash + able = _____

3. fright + en = _____

4. break + able = _____

5. invent + ion = _____

6. improve + ment=_____

7. soft + en =_____

8. direct +ion =_____

Add a suffix to make a new word.

ness	ing	er	ed	est
ful		less		ly

9. collect _____

10. care _____

11. fear _____

12 loud _____

13. fast _____

14. walk _____

15. glad _____

16. neat _____

17. thought _____

18. cheat _____

19. sleep _____

20. safe _____

Write the root word on the line. Underline the prefix, circle the suffix

21. **Ex:** <u>un</u>happi(ness) _____happy_____

22. unpacking _____

23. defrosted _____

24. repainted _____

25. incorrectly _____

26. exclaimed _____

27. imperfectly _____

28. uncomfortable _____

DAY
2

1
3
4
5

W E E K 4

Strength
Go to www.summerfitlearning.com for more Activities!

DAILY EXERCISE
Push-ups (traditional or modified)
"Stretch Before You Play!"

Instruction
Repeat 10 times

Place Value

Look at the numbers and solve the riddle.

5,650	56	506	1,560

1. I have a 6 in the ten's place. _____

2. I am greater than 5,000. _____

3. I have a 6 in the hundred's place. _____

4. I have a zero in the ten's place. _____

5. I am less than 100. _____.

Write the value of the 6.

6. 1,652 = _____   7. 68 = _____   8. 6,349 = _____   9. 206 = _____

Write the value of the 5.

10. 52 = _____   11. 1,500 = _____   12. 895 = _____   13. 5,902 = _____

Write the value of the 2.

14. 129 = _____   15. 248 = _____   16. 72 = _____   17. 2,076 = _____

18. Put these numbers in order from smallest to largest.

652	568	89	129	1,067

_____   _____   _____   _____   _____

Read the following passage on skeletons. Then answer the questions below.

The human skeleton has over 200 bones! Bones are the framework of your body. Your skeleton supports you and gives your body its shape. Your skeleton helps your body to move by giving your muscles a place to attach, these are called joints. Joints can be fixed, hinged, or ball and socket. The skeleton is also a shield. It protects soft organs such as the brain, heart, and lungs from injury.

The outside layer of bones is hard and made up of calcium and other minerals. Inside, bones are filled with a soft, fatty tissue called bone marrow. Your bone marrow has the very important job of making new blood cells for your body. The largest bone in the human body is the thigh bone, or femur. The smallest bone is called the stirrup bone, and is located inside your ear. When a bone is broken, new blood vessels grow. These eventually turn to bone. New marrow forms inside the bone and soon the bone is healed.

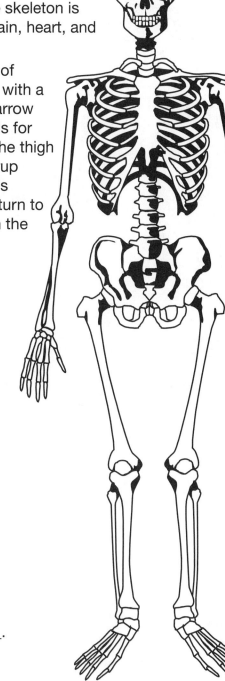

1. The body has more than _____

bones.

2. _____ makes up the hard outer

layer of bones.

3. Your skeleton protects soft organs like the

_____, _____,

and the _____.

4. The soft tissue inside your bones is called

_____.

5. Bone marrow makes new _____.

6. The largest bone is the _____.

7. Circle the plural words in the passage above. How

many did you find?_____

Aerobic
Go to www.summerfitlearning.com for more Activities!

DAILY EXERCISE
Hoops
"Stretch Before You Play!"

Instruction
Play to 11 by 1's

Be Healthy!
Instead of playing a video game play a board or card game

1

2

DAY
3

4

5

Time

Write the digital time. Add 30 minutes. What time is it now?

1.

Ex: 7:46
_____
8:16
_____

2.

_____

_____

3.

_____

_____

4.

_____

_____

5.

_____

_____

6.

_____

_____

7.

_____

_____

8.

_____

_____

Use words to write the time.

9.

Ex: 3:18 = eighteen minutes after three.

10.

2:55 = _____
_____

11.

7:29 = _____
_____

12.

9:35 = _____
_____

WEEK 4

Antonyms are words with opposite meanings, like tall and short. Match words from the box to their antonym.

clean	near	low	in	down	hot	over
happy	careful	laugh	walk	whisper	hard	dark

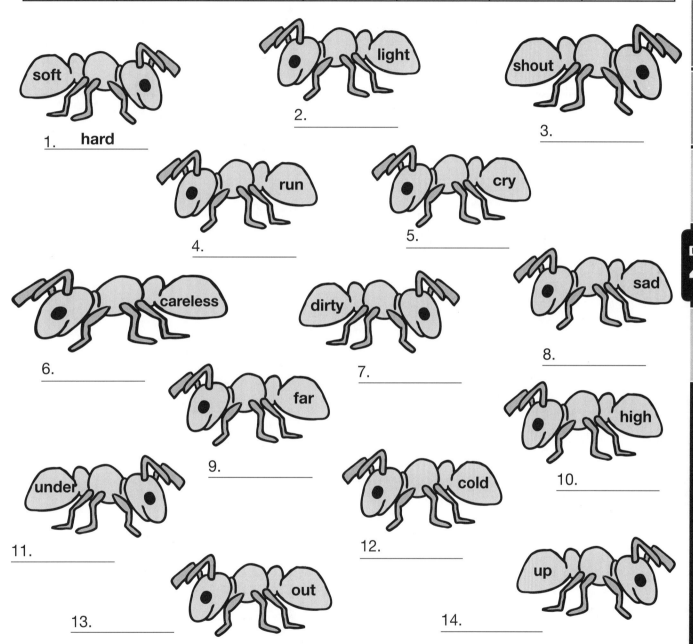

1. soft _hard_

2. light _____

3. shout _____

4. run _____

5. cry _____

6. careless _____

7. dirty _____

8. sad _____

9. far _____

10. high _____

11. under _____

12. cold _____

13. out _____

14. up _____

Think of an antonym for each underlined word.

15. A green light means <u>go</u> while a red light means _____.

16. I fell <u>asleep</u> before midnight on New Year's Eve, but my brothers stayed _____.

17. Everyone likes to <u>win</u>, but nobody likes to _____.

DAILY EXERCISE
Crunches
"Stretch Before You Play!"

Instruction
Repeat 5 times

Be Healthy!
A healthy diet helps fight off sickness.

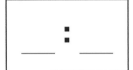

Race to the Finish

Fast Facts. Time yourself to see how fast you can complete these addition and subtraction problems.

START TIME
Ready - Set - Go!

1. 5,634	2. 4,328	3. 9,902	4. 1,200
+ 2,367	+ 2,134	+ 2,345	+ 1,052
_____	_____	_____	_____

5. 5,648	6. 6,840	7. 9,864	8. 3,452
− 3,246	- 2,420	− 6,342	− 1,260
_____	_____	_____	_____

 **STOP TIME**

 **Total time to complete**

Add 10 to each number.

9. 67 _____	11. 89 _____	13. 520 _____	15. 248 _____
10. 130 _____	12. 165 _____	14. 99 _____	16. 607 _____

Add 100 to each number.

17. 567 _____	19. 489 _____	21. 78 _____	23. 9,690 _____
18. 109 _____	20. 934 _____	22. 333 _____	24. 1,564 _____

Photo courtesy of Stephanie Lopez Cox

Self-discipline is to have control of your actions to improve and reach your goals. Self-discipline includes self-control, dedication and commitment.

Stephanie Lopez Cox works hard to reach her goals. Through self-discipline and dedication she played on the U.S. National Women's Soccer Team that won the gold medal at the 2008 Beijing Olympics. Stephanie practices very hard and is committed to doing what it takes to become the best athlete, soccer player and person she can be. Stephanie is known for her soccer skills, but also focused hard on her classes to earn a 3.76 grade point average in college. Stephanie knows what it takes to reach her goals and follows through even when it is not easy. She is disciplined as an athlete and at the same time is committed to helping others in need. Stephanie grew up in a home that fostered children; she uses the same focus and commitment that made her into a premier athlete, to help others by raising awareness for foster kids. Stephanie is dedicated to bettering the world around her through her childhood experiences and her current job as a professional athlete.

Answer true or false for each statement:

1. Stephanie doesn't work very hard. _____

2. She won a gold medal in the 2008 Olympics. _____

3. Stephanie was not a good student and got bad grades. _____

4. She tries to be a good person and a good athlete. _____

5. Stephanie helps foster children. _____

6. Stephanie only cares about herself and not others. _____.

CORE VALUES

DAY 5

WEEK 4

Choose 1 or more activities to do with your family or friends. Color today's star when you are finished. Good job!

☐ Plan to exercise together as a family. Have family walks after dinner. Hike, bike, swim, dance or play something together every day for a week. Play flashlight tag at night. Whoever gets tagged with the light is "it."

☐ Practice self-discipline when watching tv, using the computer, or playing video games. Give yourself an amount of time to play and then stick to it. When your time is up, go play outside, read a book, or spend time with family and friends.

☐ Draw a comic strip about self-discipline vs. no discipline.

Core Value Book List
Read More About Self-Discipline

The Book of Virtues
By William Bennet

Sign of the Beaver
By Elizabeth George Speare

From the Mixed Up Files of Mrs. Basil E. Frankweiler
By E. L. Konigsburg

Reading Extension Activities at SummerFitLearning.com

Let's Talk About It

Have discussions with your child about the importance of self-discipline in the many areas of their life. Role play different situations with your child and practice ways to show self-control with diet, exercise, school, video games and things such as the internet. Talk about how it feels when they lose control as opposed to how they feel when they keep control. Use the story of Stephanie Lopez Cox as an example of the focus, drive and determination it takes to excel at a specific sport or area of interest.

Play Time!
Choose a Game or Activity to Play for 60 minutes today!

YOU CHOOSE

_____

Write down which game or activity you played today!

Be Healthy!
Listen to your body. If you feel full, it's ok to stop eating!

WEEK 5

Skills of the Week

- ✔ Sentence structure
- ✔ Division
- ✔ Map skills
- ✔ Coordinate points
- ✔ Syllables
- ✔ Addition
- ✔ Subtraction
- ✔ Multiplication
- ✔ Division
- ✔ Measurement conversion
- ✔ The water cycle
- ✔ Identifying triangles

Weekly Value Kindness

Princess Diana

Kindness is caring about people, animals and the earth. It is looking for ways to help others.

Being nice to others catches on. When people are nice to each other they feel better about themselves and others. Small things make a big difference so when you smile, lend a helping hand and show concern for others, you are making the world a better place.

GET FIT TIME!

Play 60 Every Day!
Run, jump, dance and have fun outside every day for 60 minutes!

Weekly Extension Activities at SummerFitLearning.com

Kindness In Action!
Color the star each day you show kindness through your own actions.

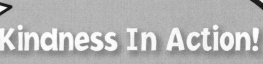

WEEK 5

Color the ⭐ As You Complete Your Daily Task

	Day 1	Day 2	Day 3	Day 4	Day 5
MIND	⭐	⭐	⭐	⭐	⭐
BODY	⭐	⭐	⭐	⭐	⭐
DAILY READING	⭐ 20 minutes	⭐ 20 minutes	⭐ 20 minutes	⭐ 20 minutes	⭐ 20 minutes

You can do it!

"I am kind"

_____
Print Name

Rewrite the sentences using correct punctuation and capitalization.

1. joseph had a sleepover with his friends Brendan Jacob and sam

_____

_____

2. i am going to visit my friend isabella in san diego california

_____

_____

3. ouch a mosquito bit me on the leg

_____

_____

4. christmas is my favorite holiday said beth

_____

_____

5. mom packed us a delicious picnic lunch of sandwiches chips carrot sticks and cookies

_____

_____

6. grandmas favorite hobby is water skiing on bear lake

_____

_____

Combine the two sentences to make one sentence.

7. Jonathan went to the circus on Saturday. Noah went to the circus on Saturday.

_____

_____

8. Amy watered the plants in the garden. Amy pulled the weeds in the garden.

_____

_____

9. Ants use their antennae to smell and touch. Ants use their antennae to find food.

_____

_____

DAY
1

2

3

4

5

WEEK 5

DAILY EXERCISE
Joggin for Fitness 10
"Stretch Before You Play!"

Instruction
Jog 10 minutes in place or outside

DAY 1

Dividing

Draw an array then write a division sentence. Solve the equation.

25 triangles in 5 rows

Divide.

1. $48 \div 6 =$ _____

2. $30 \div 5 =$ _____

3. $16 \div 4 =$ _____

4. $27 \div 9 =$ _____

5. $42 \div 6 =$ _____

6. $81 \div 9 =$ _____

7. $24 \div 6 =$ _____

8. $40 \div 8 =$ _____

9. $28 \div 7 =$ _____

Divide

10. $6 \overline{\smash{)}32}$

11. $7 \overline{\smash{)}427}$

12. $8 \overline{\smash{)}78}$

13. $2 \overline{\smash{)}64}$

14. $4 \overline{\smash{)}95}$

15. $5 \overline{\smash{)}795}$

16. $3 \overline{\smash{)}654}$

17. $3 \overline{\smash{)}2,532}$

WEEK 5

Kindness

Use the map of the Western United States of America to answer the questions.

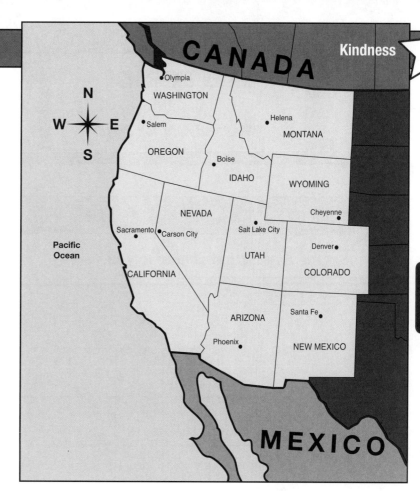

1. What state is East of Oregon?

_____

2. What is the capital of Washington?

_____

3. Salt Lake City is the capital of what state?

_____

4. Begin in Nevada, go east one state and then directly south. What state are you in?

_____

5. What country is USA's neighbor to the North?_____

6. Which Western state is the biggest? _____

7. What ocean borders California? _____

8. What is the capital of Oregon? _____

9. What are the five states that share a border with Arizona? _____

_____

10. The capital of this state is Santa Fe? _____

Strength

DAILY EXERCISE
Can Do
"Stretch Before You Play!"

Instruction
Repeat 10 times

Be Healthy!
Wash your hands before, during and after cooking food.

1

DAY 2

3

4

5

WEEK 5

Number Pairs

Connect the dots. What shape do you see?

Example: 2 across, 6 up

2, 7
3, 5
3, 8
4, 8
5, 7
6, 8
7, 8
8, 7
8, 6
7, 5
6, 4
5, 3
4, 4

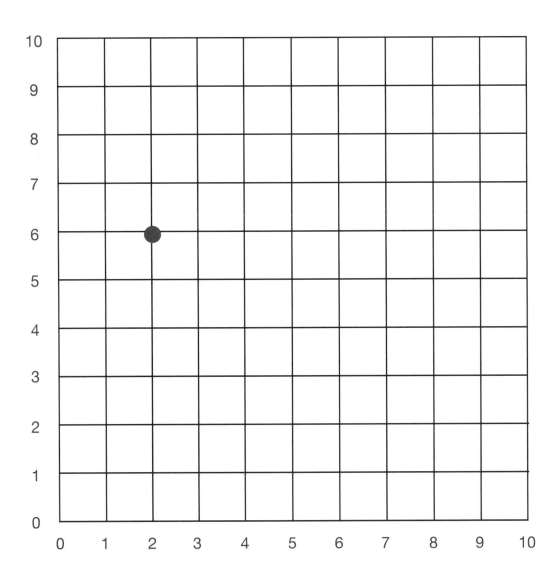

Connect the dots, what shape do you see? _____

Syllable Sleuth

A syllable is a part of a word with a distinct vowel sound (a,e,i,o,u). The number of times you hear a vowel is the number of syllables you hear.

Look at each word. Write the number of vowels you see, the number of vowels you hear, and how many syllables the word has.

Word	Vowels Seen	Vowels Heard	Number of Syllables
1. Ex: monkey	2	2	2
2. hippopotamus			
3. wolf			
4. anteater			
5. alligator			
6. tiger			
7. elephant			
8. zebra			
9. rhinoceros			

Circle where would you look to find the number of syllables in a word?

dictionary	encyclopedia	atlas

In each row, circle the word that I divided into syllables correctly.

10. b-an-ana	ba-na-na	ban-an-a
11. be-cause	bec-ause	b-e-cause
12. fl-ow-ers	fl-ower-s	flow-ers
13. neigh-bor-ly	ne-igh-borl-y	neigh-bo-rly
14. wood-pecker	wood-peck-er	wood-pe-cker

Divide each word into syllables.

15. sweater _____   17. realize _____

16. bookcase _____   18. happiness _____

Aerobic

Go to www.summerfitlearning.com for more Activities!

DAILY EXERCISE
Capture the Flag
"Stretch Before You Play!"

Instruction
Get Your Family and Friends to Play

Be Healthy!
Say "Please" when asking someone to do something for you.

1
2
DAY 3
4
5

WEEK 5

Mixed Practice

Add, subtract, multiply, or divide.

1.   234
      x 21

2.   3,029
      - 1,652

3.   2,432
      + 3,879

4.   809
      x 52

5.   6,723
      x 15

6.   9,422
      - 6,830

7.   2,652
      x 130

8.   2) 1,470

Fill in the blanks to convert the measurements.

9. 1 ft. = _____ in.

12. 1 yd. = _____ ft.

15. 1 hr. = _____ min.

10. 1 da. = _____ hr.

13. 1 qt. = _____ pt.

16. 1 yd. = _____ in.

11. 1 week = _____ da.

14. 4 qt. = _____ gal.

17. 1 pt. = _____ c.

The Water Cycle

Kindness

Have you ever stood in the rain and let the raindrops fall onto your head and trickle down your face? Did you ever wonder where this water comes from? Every day the heat from the sun evaporates water from oceans, ponds, and lakes. When the sun heats up the earth, the warm air rises and begins to cool. This cooling of the air causes cloud to form and is called condensation. Condensation is the state of water when it changes from a gas to a liquid.

When these clouds reach colder air rain, snow, hail, or sleet fall to the earth and the process of evaporation begins again. This state of water when it falls to the earth is precipitation. The earth and air are constantly exchanging water with each other. This is called the water cycle.

Answer the questions below. Circle the correct answer, write it in the blank.

1. The source of energy that heats the earth is _____.

clouds	moon	rain	sun

2. Rain, snow, hail, and sleet are forms of _____.

condensation	precipitation	energy	wind

3. The state of water when it changes from a gas to a liquid is called_____.

precipitation	rain	condensation	ice

4. The earth uses the same water over and over again.

This is called the _____ cycle.

water	sun	fire	tree

On a separate piece of paper, draw a diagram to show the water cycle.

- The sun evaporates water from the earth.
- Water condenses and forms clouds.
- Precipitation falls from the clouds in the form of rain, snow, hail, or sleet.
- Water flows back to the lakes, rivers, and oceans.

DAY 4

WEEK 5

1 2 3 5

Strength
Go to www.summerfitlearning.com for more Activities!

DAILY EXERCISE
Sky Reach
"Stretch Before You Play!"

Instruction
Repeat 10 times, and then switch arms

Eat all your meals at the kitchen table today.

Identifying Triangles

Triangles are two dimensional shapes with three sides and three angles. There are different kinds of triangles.

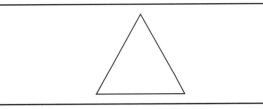

An equilateral triangle has three equal sides

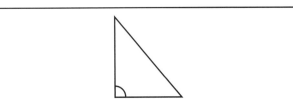

A right triangle must have one 90° angle and two angles that total exactly 90°

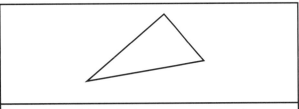

A scalene triangle has no equal sides or angles.

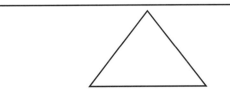

An isosceles triangle has at least two equal sides and angles.

1.	2.	3.	4.
5.	6.	7.	8.

1 2 3 DAY 4 5

74 © Summer Fit

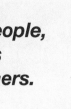

Kindness is caring about people, animals, and the earth. It is looking for ways to help others.

Princess Diana of Wales was a modern day princess with a big heart. She devoted her time to charity work and to helping people all over the world. Princess Diana gave selflessly to others in her work with the unloved, the homeless, the sick, and the abandoned. A hero is someone who makes the world a better place and Princess Diana did that. She thought of others before herself and used her fame and power to help those in need. Princess Diana had a special way of making ordinary people feel extraordinary. She was admired by people around the world for her generous smile and open heart and made everyone feel as important to the world as she was.

1. Why was Princess Diana admired around the world?

_____

_____

2. Look up the following words in the dictionary and write the definitions.

Humanitarian: _____

_____

Extraordinary: _____

_____

Choose 1 or more activities to do with your family or friends. Color today's star when you are finished. Good job!

☐ Random acts of Kindness (RAK) are kind deeds done for people who aren't expecting it. Make buttons out of paper that have the letters RAK on them. Pass them out to your friends and family after doing a kind deed for them. Tell them to "pay it forward" and pass the button on to someone else.

☐ Make care packages for the homeless shelter with your family. Include things we take for granted but are needed items such as toothpaste, toothbrushes, deodorant, soap, and shampoo.

☐ Play "10 good things game" with your friends or family. Take turns saying at least 10 nice things about a person.

Core Value Book List
Read More About Kindness

Bully on the Bus
By Carl W. Bosch

What a Wimp
By Carol Carrick

Fourth Grade Rats
By Jerry Spinelli

Reading Extension Activities at SummerFitLearning.com

Let's Talk About It

Talk to your child about how kind words and unkind words affect others. Explain to them the difference. Look for opportunities to catch your child being kind and praise them when they are. Actively promote kindness and kind acts in your household and encourage your child to do the same in their classroom.

Play Time!
Choose a Game or Activity to Play for 60 minutes today!

YOU CHOOSE

_____

Write down which game or activity you played today!

Be Healthy!
Ask your parents if you can do something for them.

WEEK 6

Skills of the Week

✔ Table of contents
✔ Fractions as decimals and decimals as fractions
✔ Bats
✔ Mixes practice
✔ Adjectives and adverbs
✔ Comparing numbers
✔ Subject and predicate
✔ Temperature

Weekly Value Courage

Rosa Parks

Courage means doing the right thing even when it is difficult and you are afraid. It means to be brave.

It can be a lot easier to do the right thing when everybody else is doing it, but it can be a lot harder to do it on our own or when nobody is looking. Remember who you are and stand up for what you believe in when it is easy and even more so when it is hard.

GET FIT TIME!

Play 60 Every Day!
Run, jump, dance and have fun outside every day for 60 minutes!

Weekly Extension Activities at SummerFitLearning.com

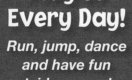

Courage In Action!
Color the star each day you show Courage through your own actions.

WEEK 6
HEALTHY MIND + HEALTHY BODY

Color the ⭐ As You Complete Your Daily Task

	Day 1	Day 2	Day 3	Day 4	Day 5
MIND	⭐	⭐	⭐	⭐	⭐
BODY	⭐	⭐	⭐	⭐	⭐
DAILY READING	⭐	⭐	⭐	⭐	⭐
	20 minutes	20 minutes	20 minutes	20 minutes	20 minutes

You can do it!

"I am brave"

_____
Print Name

The table of contents is found at the beginning of a book. The table of contents lists the chapters and the page on which they start.

Look at the table of contents above and answer the question below.

1. What would you read about in chapter 2? _____

2. What chapter would you read to learn about fossils?_____

3. Where would you learn about equipment for rock collecting? _____

4. What page is the identification guide on?_____

5. What page does the chapter on crystals begin on? _____

6. What is the shortest chapter? _____

Write the contraction for each set of words. Don't forget the apostrophe.

7. he will _____   8. can not _____   9. you are _____

10. I am _____   11. they have _____   12. she is _____

13. has not _____   14. we will _____   15. we are _____

16. is not _____   17. they are _____   18. will not _____

DAILY EXERCISE
Happy Feet
"Stretch Before You Play!"

Instruction
Ask your parents to walk with you after dinner

DAY 1

Fractions

Write each fraction as a decimal.

1. **Ex.** 8/10 = 0.8

2. 7/10 = _____

3. 75/100 = _____

4. 9/10 = _____

5. 5/10 = _____

6. 3/10 = _____

7. 10/100 = _____

8. 90/100 = _____

Write each decimal as a fraction.

9. **Ex.** .25 = 25/100 = 1/4

10. 0.6 = _____

11. 0.2 = _____

12. 0.5 = _____

13. 0.4 = _____

14. 0.75 = _____

15. 0.4 = _____

16. 0.9 = _____

17. 0.15 = _____

18. 0.35 = _____

The numerator is the top number of a fraction and tells how many equal parts are used. The denominator is the bottom number and tells how many equal parts in all.

$$\frac{1}{2} \quad \begin{array}{l} = \text{numerator} \\ = \text{denominator} \end{array}$$

Look at the fractions in each pair. Circle the fraction with the greater value.

19. 1/5 or 1/6

20. 1/2 or 1/4

21. 1/3 or 2/3

22. 4/5 or 1/5

23. 1/100 or 1/10

24. 1/7 or 4/7

WEEK 6

Read the passage on bats then answer the questions below.

There are over a thousand different kinds of bats. Although they can be found all over the world, most of the world's bat population lives near the equator because of the warm climate. The largest bat has a wingspan of almost six feet, while the smallest bat is about as big as a bumblebee with just a five-inch wingspan. A bat's wingspan is the measurement from the tip of one wing to the tip of the other while fully extended.

Most bats are brown, but they can also be other colors, like black, white, red, and even yellow. Bats like to live in colonies with many other bats. They make their homes in caves, trees, tunnels, and attics. Bats are nocturnal, which means they are active at night and sleep during the day. While sleeping, bats hang upside down by their toes with their wings wrapped around them for protection.

Bats are mammals and feed their young with milk. Even though they can fly, bats are not birds. However, they are the only mammal that can fly like a bird. Bats have extremely good hearing and use a kind of sonar called echolocation to navigate the dark and hunt for food. Most bats eat insects, but some also eat rodents, fish, fruit, and even other bats. The famous vampire bat feed on the blood of cattle and birds. Because bats eat so many insects they are very important to the environment and help keep the insect population under control.

Write T if the statement is true and F if it is false. Correct the false statements.

1. Bats prefer a warmer climate. _____

2. Bats are nocturnal. _____

3. Most bats like to live alone. _____

4. Bats can be many different colors. _____

5. Bats are birds. _____

6. Bats are mammals. _____

7. Bats use their eyes to see in the dark. _____

8. Most bats don't eat insects. _____

9. The vampire bat feed on the blood of cattle and birds. _____

Strength

Go to www.summerfitlearning.com for more Activities!

DAILY EXERCISE
Bottle Lift
"Stretch Before You Play!"

Instruction
Repeat 10 times

Be Healthy!
Ask your parents to buy 1% or skim milk instead of whole milk.

1 **DAY 2** **3** **4** **5**

WEEK 6

Number Practice

Divide.

1. How many 2's in 12? ___6___

2. How many 8's in 64? _____

3. How many 6's in 54? _____

4. How many 12's in 36? _____

5. How many 5's in 60? _____

6. How many 4's in 40? _____

7. How many 3's in 27? _____

8. How many 7's in 28? _____

Write the numbers in order from least to greatest.

9. 806 860 680 86 _____, _____, _____, _____.

10. 456 540 154 654 _____, _____, _____, _____.

11. 87 78 107 70 _____, _____, _____, _____.

12. 555 505 450 105 _____, _____, _____, _____.

Find the pattern and continue each row.

13. 68, 65, 62, _____, _____, _____, _____, _____ .

14. 7, 14, 21, _____, _____, _____, _____, _____ .

15. 80, 78, 76, _____, _____, _____, _____, _____ .

16. 115, 120, 125, _____, _____, _____, _____, _____ .

17. 200, 190, 180, _____, _____, _____, _____, _____ .

18. 56, 58, 60, _____, _____, _____, _____, _____ .

Add 100 to each number.

19. 32 _____   3,270 _____   250 _____   24 _____

20. 576 _____   5,234 _____   345 _____   1,607 _____

Subtract 100 from each number.

21. 789 _____   198 _____   560 _____   351 _____

22. 2,560 _____   1,893 _____   2,990 _____   330 _____

An adjective describes a noun. An adverb describes a verb. While many adverbs end in ly many adjectives do too.

Circle each ly word and say whether it is an adjective or an adverb.

1. The children waited patiently in line for the movie. _____

2. The sleepy baby cried loudly on his mother's lap. _____

3. The sun shone brightly in the sky. _____

4. The farmer worked tirelessly plowing the fields. _____

5. The girl's curly hair bounced as she ran. _____

6. The smelly garbage sat in the can for days. _____

7. The soldiers fought bravely for their country. _____

8. The wind gently rustled the leaves in the trees. _____

9. The friendly clerk offered to help carry our packages. _____

10. We ran quickly to the car to get out of the rain. _____

Circle the adjective in each sentence and write the noun it modifies on the line.

Ex. The (giant) pumpkin was rolled onto the truck. <u>pumpkin</u>

11. The beautiful ballerina danced across the stage. _____

12. The shy boy shrugged his shoulders. _____

13. We picked a pretty bouquet of flowers for our grandma. _____

14. The fluffy kitten jumped onto my lap. _____

15. The marching band played three songs at the game. _____

16. The patient librarian read the book to a large group of toddlers. _____

Use an adjective and an adverb to complete each sentence.

Ex. The <u>green</u> snake slithered slowly behind the rock.

17. The _____ man walked _____ through the park.

18. The _____ spider skittered _____ up the wall.

19. The _____ band played _____ at the concert.

20. The _____ children _____ opened their presents.

Sidebar: 1 2 **DAY 3** 4 5 WEEK 6

DAILY EXERCISE
Let's Roll
"Stretch Before You Play!"

Instruction
Ride for 10 Minutes

1
2
DAY
3
4
5

WEEK 6

Compare the Numbers

Write > ,<, or = for each pair.

1. **Ex.** 3 x 6 _> _ 10 + 4

2. $3.56 _____ $3.65

3. 7 x 6 _____ 9 x 5

4. 6 in. _____ 6 ft.

5. 3 + 4 _____ 3 x 4

6. 42 ÷ 7 _____ 36 ÷ 9

7. 40 ÷5 _____ 3 x 4

8. 4 x 4 _____ 2 x 8

9. 20 ÷ 4 _____ 9 - 3

10. 1 x 0 _____ 1 x 1

11. 5,020 _____ 5,202

12. 10 ÷5 _____ 20 ÷ 10

13. 1/2 _____ 1/4

14. .50 _____ 1/2

15. 9 x 11 _____ 100 - 10

16. 8 x 9 _____ 9 x 8

Fill in the blank with the best measurement, feet, inches, yards, centimeters, or miles.

17. The bookcase is 2 _____ deep.

18. Joseph's dad is 6 _____ tall.

19. The football field is 100 _____ long.

20. The library is 5 _____ from the house.

21. The pencil is 4 _____ long.

22. The bug is 2 _____ long.

Circle the greater of each pair.

23.	quart	cup
24.	inch	centimeter
25.	mile	yard
26.	day	week

27.	minute	second
28.	ounce	pound
29.	yard	foot
30.	dime	nickel

All good sentences have a subject and a predicate. The subject of a sentence tells who or what the sentence is about. The predicate modifies or tells about the subject. The subject and predicate can be just one word or more than one word.

Circle the subject of each sentence and underline the predicate.

Ex. The (energetic monkeys) howled in the trees.

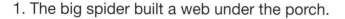

1. The big spider built a web under the porch.

2. Amanda and Rachel visited the Doll and Toy Museum.

3. The space alien landed his ship in the field.

4. Joe and his brother played in the chess tournament.

5. The children played in the sandbox.

6. The moon and stars shone brightly in the sky.

7. The horse galloped across the field.

8. We rode the bus to the zoo.

Write two complete sentences. Be sure to include the subject and the predicate.

9. _____

_____

_____ .

10. _____

_____

_____ .

Strength
Go to www.summerfitlearning.com for more Activities!

DAILY EXERCISE
Chop n Squat
"Stretch Before You Play!"

Instruction
Repeat 10 times

1

2

3

DAY 4

5

Temperature

The boiling point of water is 212° Fahrenheit or 100° Celsius

The freezing point of water is 32° Fahrenheit or 0° Celsius

Read each thermometer and write the temperature.

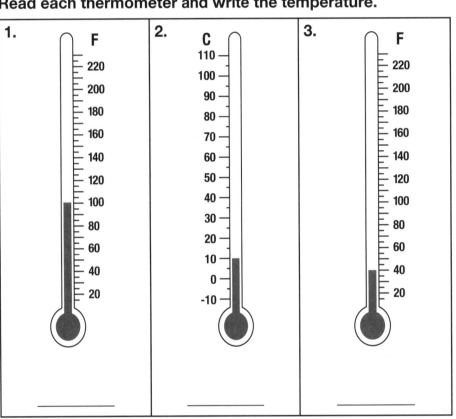

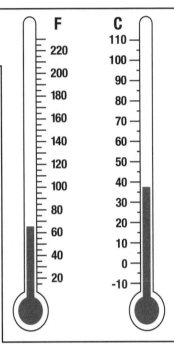

1. F

2. C

3. F

_____   _____   _____

4. The boiling point of water is _____ ° Fahrenheit.

5. The freezing point of water is _____ ° Celsius.

6. The instrument used to measure temperature is called

a _____.

7. Color the thermometer to the right to show the temperature 64° F.

F

WEEK 6

Courage means doing the right thing even when it is difficult and you are afraid. It means to be brave.

An Act of Courage

Rosa Parks had always dreamed things would be different. She dreamed of a day when there would be freedom for everyone and one day she stood up for everything she believed in. On that day in early December, 1955, Rosa got on the bus and instead of sitting in the back where the black people were supposed to sit, she sat in the front of the bus. The front of the bus was only reserved for white people and when the bus driver asked her to get up, Rosa refused. The police came and Rosa was arrested. Her courage made other people want to fight for freedom too and there was a boycott. The boycott meant that no black people rode the busses. Finally, the rules for riding the bus were changed and black and white people could sit wherever they wanted. Rosa is a hero because she stood up for what was right even though it was hard and even though she stood alone. Her act of courage helped other people want to stand up for what was right too.

Design an American postage stamp that shows why Rosa Parks is a hero. Color your stamp.

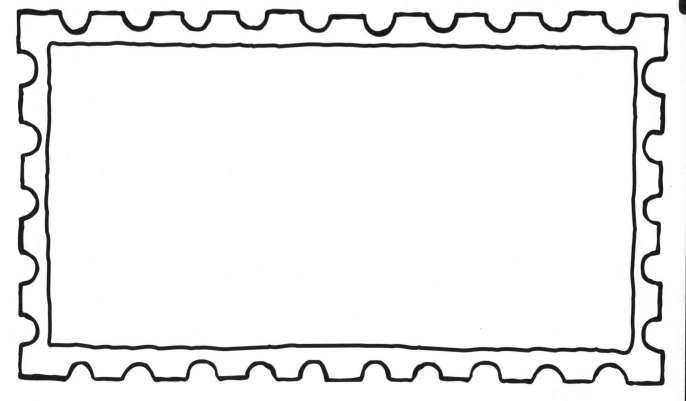

Choose 1 or more activities to do with your family or friends. Color today's star when you are finished. Good job!

☐ Francis Scott Key wrote the USA's National Anthem, "The Star Spangled Banner," after seeing the American flag still waving after an attack by the British. Look up the lyrics to the song and think about the courage of all the people who have fought for America's freedom.

☐ Many people in our community show great courage every day as they work to help and protect us. Firefighters, police officers, and soldiers are just a few. Write a letter to one of them thanking them for the courage they show every day.

☐ Find a magazine or newspaper article about someone who performed a courageous or brave act. Read about them and re-tell the story to your family.

Core Value Book List
Read More About Courage

Call It Courage
By Armstrong Sperry

Little House Books
By Laura Ingalls Wilder

The Castle in the Attic
By Elizabeth Winthrop

Reading Extension Activities at SummerFitLearning.com

Let's Talk About It

Bullying is widespread. It can have a lasting impact and leave emotional scars. Talk to your kids about bullying and help them have the tools they need to stand up to bullies or to stop being the bully. Some tactics you can try at home: teach your kids that when teasing becomes hurtful and unkind it has crossed the line into bullying. Teach your kids to treat others with kindness and respect and to be tolerant of each other's differences. Encourage good behavior; catch them being good and praise them. Most importantly, set a good example, our children may not always do what we say but they will follow what we do. Let your kids know that bullying is unacceptable and it is just as unacceptable to stand by and watch someone being bullied.

Play Time!
Choose a Game or Activity to Play for 60 minutes today!

YOU CHOOSE

_____

Write down which game or activity you played today!

Be Healthy!
Try to eat 3 different vegetables today!

1 2 3 4

DAY 5

WEEK 6

WEEK 7

Skills of the Week

✔ Good nutrition
✔ Money math
✔ Similes
✔ Average
✔ Solving for x
✔ United states map skills
✔ Place value
✔ Mixed practice
✔ Elapsed time
✔ Verb "to be"
✔ Intersecting
✔ Parallel, and perpendicular lines

Weekly Value Respect

Respect is honoring yourself and others. It is behaving in a way that makes life peaceful and orderly.

Mahatma Gandhi

Sometimes we forget to appreciate that every person is unique and different. All of us want to be accepted and appreciated for who we are. Try to treat others the way that you want to be treated, even when it is difficult.

GET FIT TIME!

Play 60 Every Day!

Run, jump, dance and have fun outside every day for 60 minutes!

Weekly Extension Activities at SummerFitLearning.com

Respect In Action!

Color the star each day you show respect through your own actions.

Color the ⭐ As You Complete Your Daily Task

	Day 1	Day 2	Day 3	Day 4	Day 5
MIND	⭐	⭐	⭐	⭐	⭐
BODY	⭐	⭐	⭐	⭐	⭐
DAILY READING	⭐ 20 minutes	⭐ 20 minutes	⭐ 20 minutes	⭐ 20 minutes	⭐ 20 minutes

You can do it!

"I am respectful"

_____

Print Name

Eating healthy foods allows your body to get the nutrients it needs to function and grow. Making healthy choices and eating a balanced diet help give you the energy you need to learn, work, and play. Protein like beans and lean meats help your muscles grow and stay strong. Grains like bread, pasta and cereal are an important source of fiber that helps you digest your food and give you energy. Dairy products such as milk and cheese provide calcium for strong bones and teeth. Fruits and vegetables are all natural and are loaded with the vitamins and minerals your body needs. While sweets and fatty foods such as cake and french fries may taste good, they should be eaten only once in a while and in small amounts. These foods are high in calories and have no nutritional value.

Study the image from ChooseMyPlate.gov, then think of foods that fit into each category and write them in the correct column. An example of each has been done for you.

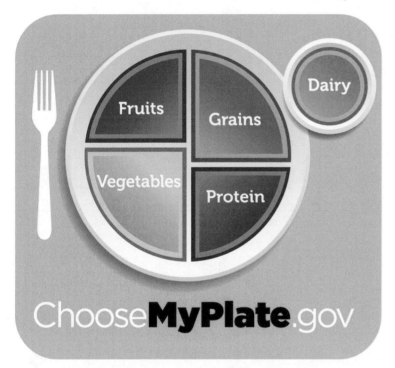

Tips for healthy eating:

- Drink a full glass of water at every meal and throughout the day.

- Choose fruits and vegetables for snacks.

- Ask your mom or dad if you can help plan healthy meals for the week, shop with them for healthy foods, and help prepare the healthy meals.

- Try to eat dinner as a family at least 3 times a week, at the table and with the tv off.

Write three examples of each kind of food.

protein	dairy	fruits	vegetables	grains	sweets
peanut butter	milk	peach	broccoli	oatmeal	cake

Aerobic
Go to www.summerfitlearning.com for more Activities!

DAILY EXERCISE
Speed
"Stretch Before You Play!"

Instruction
Run 2 Blocks

Be Healthy!
Do not interrupt when someone is talking to you.

DAY 1

2 3 4 5

WEEK 7

Rounding Money

Round each amount to the nearest dollars.
Ex. $1.20 = $1.00

1. $.85 = ___$1.00___

2. $1.76 = _____

3. $1.56 = _____

4. $19.59 = _____

5. $13.45 = _____

6. $ 5.98 = _____

7. $9.43 = _____

8. $12.77 = _____

9. $16.21 = _____

10. $8.09 = _____

How much money?

11. 2 quarters   _____._____
     3 nickels   _____._____
     23 pennies + _____._____

     $ _____._____

12. 3 quarters   _____._____
     12 dimes   _____._____
     4 nickels   + _____._____

     $ _____._____

Add or subtract to find the answer.

13. $24.00
    + $17.50

14. $85.00
    - $36.25

15. $23.86
    + $14.72

16. $260.38
    - $158.24

17. $ 83.50
        x 2

18. $24.54
         x 5

---

92 © Summer Fit

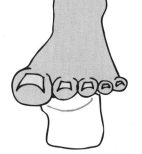
A **simile** is a comparison made between two unlike things. The word simile comes from a Latin word that means sameness. **Similes** can make our writing and speaking more interesting. We can easily recognize a **simile** because it will use the words " like" or "as". For example: "as soft as a marshmallow" or "runs like the wind."

Match each phrase on the left with a phrase on the right to complete a simile.

1. As big as a...	baby
2. As cute as a...	old shoe
3. They fought like...	button
4. As hard as a...	hyena
5. I slept like a...	rock
6. As flat as a...	glove
7. It fits like a...	house
8. He laughs like a...	pancake
9. As comfortable as an...	cats and dogs

Choose 3 of the phrases from the first column and make up your own comparison for the second phrase.

10. _____

11. _____

12. _____

DAY 2

1
3
4
5

WEEK 7

Strength

Go to www.summerfitlearning.com for more Activities!

DAILY EXERCISE
Side Step
"Stretch Before You Play!"

Instruction
Repeat 5 times in each direction

Averages

Sam's basketball team scored the following points for their June games. What was the average score?

5, 7, 9, 7, 10, 8, 10

Ex. $5 + 7 + 9 + 7 + 10 + 8 + 10 = 56$ $56 \div 7 = 8$ Average score = 8

Use addition and division to find the averages.

1. $1 + 4 + 2 + 7 + 3 + 8 + 2 + 5 =$ _____

2. $8 + 3 + 6 + 3 + 8 + 2 + 8 + 2 =$ _____

3. $7 + 5 + 9 + 7 + 2 + 4 + 8 + 6 =$ _____

4. $6 + 3 + 7 + 4 + 5 + 4 + 6 =$ _____

5. $3 + 8 + 6 + 7 + 5 + 9 + 4 =$ _____

6. Daniel bought an apple for .50 cents. He paid with a dollar.

How much change did he get back? _____

7. Emma bought a cookie for .75 cents. She paid with a dollar.

How much change did she get back. _____

Solve and check.

8. $x + 6 = 10 + 5 - 1$ x = _____

9. $x - 4 = 12 \div 3$ x = _____

Work the problems. Solve within the parentheses first and pay attention to the signs.

10. $2 \times (42 \div 7) + 8 =$ _____

11. $9 \times (2 + 3) - 4 =$ _____

12. $16 - (3 \times 3) + 6 =$ _____

13. $5 + (6 \times 2) - 3 =$ _____

Here is a map of the United States of America. Use a globe or an atlas to answer the questions below.

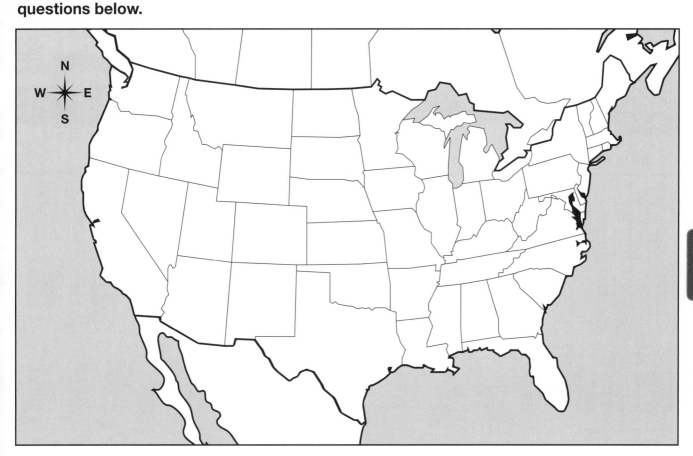

1. Find and label the Pacific and Atlantic Oceans.

2. Find and label the following states: California, Florida, Washington, Minnesota, Pennsylvania, Utah, and Arizona.

3. Find and label the U.S. capital.

4. Label the largest and smallest states.

4. Find and label your state and your state's capital.

5. Label the state east of Alabama.

6. Find and label the Dakotas and the Carolinas.

7. Find and locate the state with the capital Lincoln.

8. Find and label USA's neighboring countries.

Aerobic

Go to www.summerfitlearning.com for more Activities!

DAILY EXERCISE
Hopscotch
"Stretch Before You Play!"

Instruction
Play 3 Games

Be Healthy!
Drive by the drive-thru: it's hard to get healthy fast food!

Mixed Practice

Write the digits in the proper places. Read the numbers.

	Thousands	Hundreds	Tens	Ones
Ex. 543		5	4	3
1. 987				
2. 1,276				
3. 5,820				
4. 694				
5. 9,041				
6. 8,349				

Show 6 x 3 = 18 four ways.

7. _____   9. _____

8. _____   10. _____

Show 8 x 4 = 32 four ways.

11. _____   13. _____

12. _____   14. _____

15. What time is it?

_____:_____

16. What time was it 25 minutes ago?

_____:_____

© Summer Fit

The verb "be" tells what the subject of a sentence <u>is</u> or <u>was</u>. "Am," "is," and "are" tell about the subject in the <u>present</u>. "Was" and "were" tell about the subject in the <u>past</u>.

Write the form of "be" to complete each sentence.

were	are	is	was	am

1. The beach _____ a fun place to go.

2. Sand castles _____ fun to build in the sand.

3. There _____ many families at the beach last weekend.

4. My surfboard _____ a gift from my parents.

5. I _____ training to be a junior lifeguard.

Circle the verb that best completes the sentence.

6. I (is, am) nine years old.

7. Mary and Beth (are, is) best friends.

8. The dogs (was, were) barking loudly when the doorbell rang.

9. We (are, is) going to plant a garden this summer.

10. My Grandma (is, are) coming for a visit.

1
2
3

DAY 4

5

WEEK 7

Strength
Go to www.summerfitlearning.com for more Activities!

Geometry

Classify each set of lines as intersecting, parallel, or perpendicular.

1.

_____

2.

_____

3.

_____

4.

_____

5.

_____

6.

_____

How many lines of symmetry in each shape?

7. M

_____

8. H

_____

9. T

_____

10. I

_____

11. A

_____

12. X

_____

Respect is honoring yourself and others.

Mahatma Gandhi was a great political and spiritual leader of India. His name means "Great Soul" and although he was meek and humble, he demonstrated that true strength came from peace and harmony. For years he helped people stand up against unfair treatment. His "weapons" were peaceful protests, marches, and strikes. Gandhi believed that every life was valuable and worthy of respect and he worked hard to protect the rights of all people. He lived what he preached and his life was an example of how to live in peace and harmony. Gandhi taught that if you hurt another person you were really hurting yourself. He wanted people to find peaceful ways of reconciling their differences and to live in harmony with love and respect for all, even their enemies.

Antonyms are words that mean the opposite. Choose an antonym from the list to fill in each blank.

war	lose	help	weakness	worthless	arrogant

1. valuable _____

2. strength _____

3. gain _____

4. humble _____

5. peace _____

6. hurt _____

7. What lesson did Gandhi teach?

_____

_____

Choose 1 or more activities to do with your family or friends. Color today's star when you are finished. Good job!

☐ Make a list of things people do to show respect (hold the door open, look at them when they are talking, have manners, don't interrupt etc). Make a chart for yourself or your family. Keep track of how many times you do each act with a star or sticker.

☐ List some ways to respect the environment. How can you make a difference? Set up a recycling system for you family and use it. Practice ways to conserve water, electricity etc. Try to use only what you need.

☐ Make a commercial with your friends or siblings. Try to sell "RESPECT" so that others will want to use it.

Core Value Book List
Read More About Respect

The Skin You Live In
By Michael Tyler

Let's Talk About Race
By Julius Lester

Free To Be You and Me
By Marlo Thomas
and Friends

Reading Extension
Activities at
SummerFitLearning.com

Let's Talk About It

Talk with your child about self-respect and how we need to respect ourselves before we can respect others. Talk about and role-play how to show respect in different situations. The best way to teach respect is to show respect. Help them remember the saying "Do unto others as you would have them do unto you."

DAY 5

WEEK 7

1 2 3 4

Play Time!
Choose a Game or Activity to Play for 60 minutes today!

YOU CHOOSE

_____

Write down which game or activity you played today!

Be Healthy!
Clean the kitchen without being asked.

PARENT TIPS FOR WEEK 8

Skills of the Week

✔ Continents and oceans

✔ Measurement and data

✔ Verbs: past, present, and future

✔ Time and money

✔ Alphabetical order

✔ Reading a menu

✔ Writing webs

✔ Area of rectangles

Weekly Value Responsibility

Being responsible means others can depend on you. It is being accountable for what you do and for what you do not do.

Terry Fox

A lot of times it is easier to look to someone else to step forward and do the work or to blame others when it does not get done. You are smart, capable and able so try to be the person who accepts challenges and does not blame others if it does not get done.

GET FIT TIME!

Play 60 Every Day!

Run, jump, dance and have fun outside every day for 60 minutes!

Weekly Extension Activities at SummerFitLearning.com

Responsibility In Action!

Color the star each day you show responsibility through your own actions.

Color the ⭐ As You Complete Your Daily Task

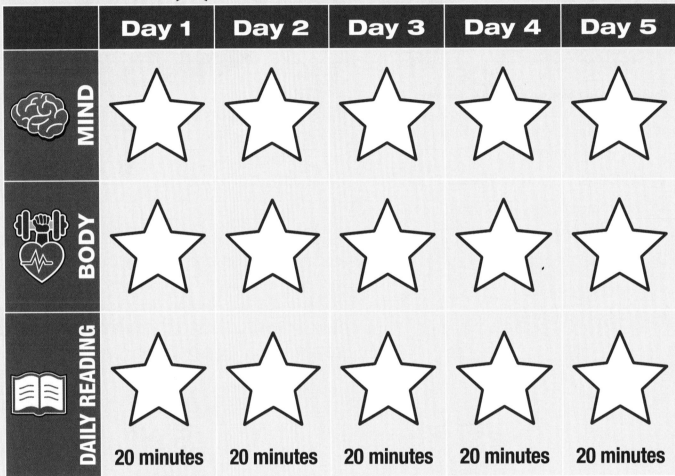

		Day 1	Day 2	Day 3	Day 4	Day 5
🧠	MIND	⭐	⭐	⭐	⭐	⭐
💪	BODY	⭐	⭐	⭐	⭐	⭐
📖	DAILY READING	⭐ 20 minutes	⭐ 20 minutes	⭐ 20 minutes	⭐ 20 minutes	⭐ 20 minutes

You can do it!

"I am responsible"

Print Name

Jacques Cousteau (1910-1997) was the world's most famous oceanographer. Cousteau combined his two loves the ocean and film-making to bring the underwater world to millions of people. He was also a great writer and inventor. Look in an encyclopedia or on the internet to find out more about this fascinating man.

DAY 1

2

3

4

5

WEEK 8

Oceans

Oceans make up more than 70% of our planet's surface and contain over 90% of the earth's water. People everywhere depend on the ocean for food and energy. There are five oceans in the world. From largest to smallest they are the Pacific Ocean, Atlantic Ocean, Indian Ocean, Southern Ocean, and Arctic Ocean. The Pacific Ocean covers nearly 1/3 of the earth's surface and is larger than the seven continents put together.

Oceanography is the study of the ocean and all that it contains. Oceanographers explore and study the ocean and all that it contains. Oceanographers explore and study the ocean to learn about its environment and all its inhabitants, plant and animal. Oceanographers use many tools to help them learn about the ocean, including satellites, submersibles, sonar devices, and current meters. With all the equipment available to them, oceanographers can study and chart parts of the ocean never explored before.

Answer the questions.

1. The oceans contain what percentage of the earth's water?

2. Name the world's five oceans from smallest to largest. _____,

_____, _____, _____, _____.

3. What is an oceanographer? _____

Look up the word <u>submersible</u> in the dictionary and write the definition.

_____

_____

Look on a globe or map to find the earth's five oceans. How quickly can you locate them?

Aerobic
Go to www.summerfitlearning.com for more Activities!

DAILY EXERCISE	Instruction	Be Healthy!
Tag	**Get your family and**	A good night's
"Stretch Before You Play!"	**friends to play**	sleep is important for everybody!

DAY 1

1+2=3

Measurement and Data

Look at the graph showing the number of cans Mr. Dean's 4th grade class collected over the school year.

Cans collected September through May

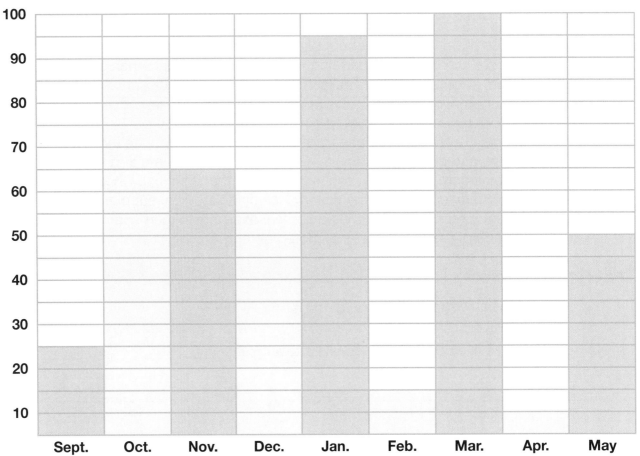

1. During which month were the most cans collected? _____

2. During which month were the fewest cans collected? _____

3. What is the average of the number of cans collected during September, October, and November? _____

4. How many more cans were collected in March than in April? _____

5. Write the amount of cans collected from least to greatest. _____

_____

6. What is the range of the cans collected (difference between most and least)? _____

Complete the sentences using verbs from the verb box.

Fill in the verbs using the past tense.

1. Last week I _____ the lawn.

2. Yesterday, I _____ pancakes for breakfast.

3. We _____ marshmallows before we put out the campfire.

4. The baby birds _____ in their nest.

VERB BOX

mow

eat

toast

chirp

Fill in the verbs using present tense.

5. When the kettle _____, will you make some tea?

6. The baby is _____ with the toy.

7. Mom is _____ dinner in the kitchen.

8. Grandma is _____ me a sweater.

VERB BOX

boil

play

cook

make

Fill in the verbs using future tense.

9. Tim _____ _____ tomorrow when he gets home.

10. I _____ _____ the ball next time .

11. The eggs _____ _____ in about 21 days.

12. I _____ _____ the piano every day.

VERB BOX

skate

catch

hatch

practice

DAY **2**

1

3

4

5

WEEK 8

Strength
Go to www.summerfitlearning.com for more Activities!

DAILY EXERCISE
Toe Taps
"Stretch Before You Play!"

Instruction
Repeat 10 times with each foot

Be Healthy!
Create a Plant Alphabet list starting with Apple.

Numbers and Math - Mixed Practice

Time Problems. Use the hands on the clocks to answer the following questions.

1.

What time was it 45 minutes ago?_____

What time will it be in 1 hour?_____

How many minutes until 9:45? _____

2.

What time will it be in 20 minutes? _____

What time was it 30 minutes ago?_____

How many minutes until 3:55? _____

3.

What time was it 45 minutes ago?_____

What time will it be in 35 minutes? _____

How many minutes until 1:00? _____

4. One play ticket costs $12.00. How much will Jacob need to buy 4 tickets?

$ _____

5. Noah bought a book for $6.87 and paid with a $10.00 bill.

How much change did he get back? $ _____ Draw the change.

Frankie could buy 4 cookies for $2.00 or 8 cookies for $3.00. Circle the better buy.

4 cookies	8 cookies

Look it up

Responsibility

Guide words appear at the top of each dictionary page and are in alphabetical order. The word on the top left is the first word on the page. The word on the top right is the last word on the page.

The guide words on a dictionary page are *fireworks* and *fishing*. Circle all the words words you would find on that page.

Fireworks	**Fishing**
firm	frame
fight	first
fish	fisherman
fishhook	fast

Number each set of words in alphabetical order

1.

snake _____

silly _____

snow _____

shovel _____

second _____

2.

hammer _____

happy _____

hare _____

heavy _____

hedge _____

3.

owl _____

order _____

open _____

odor _____

office _____

4.

dance _____

dishes _____

danger _____

door _____

direct _____

1

2

DAY 3

4

5

WEEK 8

Aerobic
Go to www.summerfitlearning.com for more Activities!

DAILY EXERCISE
Hide-and-Seek
"Stretch Before You Play!"

Instruction
Get your family and friends to play

Be Healthy!
Eat a healthy snack like popcorn!

Menu Math

Read and answer the story problems using the menu.

```
                        MENU

Hot dog  $1.25        Soda $1.00        Fries .85

Hamburger $2.00       Salad $3.00       Ice Cream $1.50
```

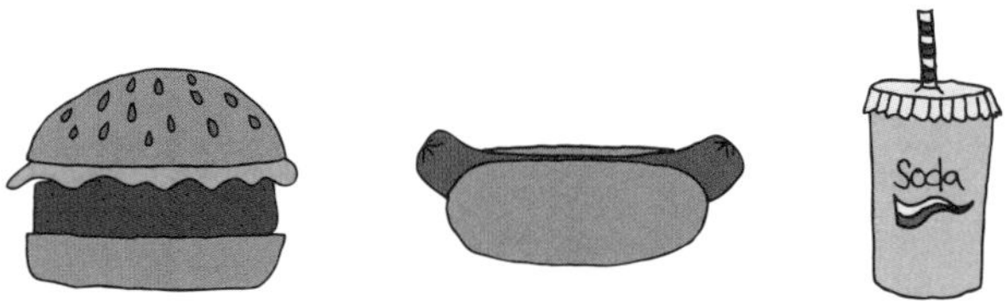

1. Sophie ordered a hot dog, fries, and a soda. How much did her order cost?_____

2. Sophie paid with $5.00. How much was her change?_____

3. Jack ordered a hamburger, salad, and ice cream. How much did his food cost? _____

4. Jack paid with a $10 bill. How much change did he get back?_____

5. Kim wants to order a salad, fries, and ice cream. If she has only $5.00 will she have

enough money? _____. If not, how much more will she need?

6. What is the most expensive item on the menu?_____

7. What is the least expensive item on the menu?_____

8. How much would two hamburgers, two orders of fries, and one ice cream cost? _____

WEEK 8

DAY 3

1 2 3 4 5

Think of a person, living or dead, who is your hero. Write their name in the center of the web above "My Hero." Fill in the other bubbles with adjectives to describe your hero.

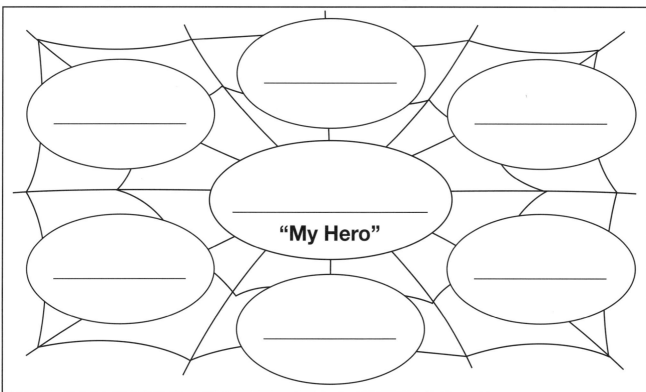

"My Hero"

Write a paragraph on your hero. Remember to include a topic sentence, supporting sentences, and a conclusion.   Use your best handwriting and watch your spelling and punctuation. Write the title on the top line.

_____

_____

_____

_____

_____

_____

_____

<u>Topic Sentence</u> tells the main idea of the paragraph.

<u>Supporting Sentences</u> give detail about the main idea.

<u>Concluding Sentences</u> sum up the paragraph or give a final thought to bring it to a clear end.

1
2
3
DAY 4
5

WEEK 8

Strength

Go to www.summerfitlearning.com for more Activities!

DAILY EXERCISE
Chin-ups
"Stretch Before You Play!"

Instruction
Repeat 2 times

Be Healthy!
Smile!

Area

To find the area of each rectangle, multiply the length by the width. Write the area on each line.

1.

4 in

3 in

Area = _____ ^{2} in

4.

12 ft

4 ft

Area = _____ ^{2} ft

2.

7 cm

5 cm

Area = _____ ^{2} cm

5.

10 m

5 m

Area = _____ ^{2} m

3.

9 ft

8 ft

Area = _____ ^{2} ft

6.

8 in

4 in

Area = _____ ^{2} in

1
2
3
DAY 4
5
WEEK 8

© Photo courtesy of the Terry Fox Foundation

Responsibility is to do what you think you should, for yourself and others, even when it is difficult.

Terrance Stanley Fox was a very good athlete. His favorite sport was basketball but he also played rugby, golf and ran cross country in high school. Sadly, Terry lost one of his legs because he got cancer. He felt it was his responsibility to do all that he could for other people with cancer and even though it was very hard, he set off to run across Canada with an artificial leg to raise money for cancer research. He called his run the Marathon of Hope. When he started to run not many people knew about Terry or what he was doing but now people all over the world participate or take part in the event. The annual Terry Fox Run has become the world's largest one-day fund raiser for cancer research.

www.terryfox.org

When Terry Fox was diagnosed with cancer he could have given up, but instead he inspired us and gave others hope.

Fill in the blanks with words from the story.

1. Terrance Stanley Fox was an athlete from _____.

2. He had to have one of his legs amputated because of _____.

3. Terrance felt it was his responsibility to raise money for cancer_____.

4. He ran across Canada with an artificial leg to raise _____.

5. Terrance called his marathon the Marathon of _____.

6. Look up the word amputate in the dictionary and write down its meaning.

amputate: _____

_____

Choose 1 or more activities to do with your family or friends. Color today's star when you are finished. Good job!

☐ What do you think is the most responsible job in the world? Interview someone who has this job and write a news story.

☐ Think about your responsibilities to your community. Being responsible means we care about others and their well-being. What are some ways you can support others in your own community?

☐ Being responsible means "owning" your behavior and the consequences. Keep a behavior journal for one week. Keep track of situations that come up during the week in which you have a chance to act responsibly or irresponsibly. Write them down and how you handled them. At the end of the week show your journal to an adult and ask for feedback and suggestions.

Core Value Book List
Read More About Responsibility

Stone Fox
By John R. Gardiner

Dakota Spring
By D. Anne Love

The Sign of the Beaver
By Elizabeth G. Speare

Reading Extension
Activities at
SummerFitLearning.com

Let's Talk About It

Discuss with your child the importance of being responsible in what they say and what they do. Talk with them about Terry Fox and how he chose to be responsible for the well-being of others. Help them understand that responsibility is a choice. Role-play some situations your child might face in his/her everyday life. Switch up the scenarios so they can see how different situations would turn out based on if they were responsible or not.

Play Time!

Choose a Game or Activity to Play for 60 minutes today!

YOU CHOOSE

_____
Write down which game or activity you played today!

Be Healthy!
Drink water instead of soda.

1

2

3

4

DAY
5

WEEK 8

PARENT TIPS FOR WEEK 9

Skills of the Week

✔ Word endings
✔ Adding and subtracting fractions
✔ Sentence fragments
✔ Articles "a" and "an"
✔ Multiplication
✔ Ecosystems
✔ Division
✔ Multiples of 10
✔ Creative writing
✔ Lines of symmetry

Weekly Value Perseverance

Bethany Hamilton

Perseverance means not giving up or giving in when things are difficult. It means you try again when you fail.

Sometimes it is easy to forget that a lot of things in life require patience and hard work. Do not give up because it is hard to accomplish a task or to get something that we want. Focus on your goal and keep working hard. It is through this experience that you will accomplish what you want.

GET FIT TIME!

Play 60 Every Day!
Run, jump, dance and have fun outside every day for 60 minutes!

Weekly Extension Activities at SummerFitLearning.com

Perseverance In Action!
Color the star each day you show perseverance through your own actions.

WEEK 9

Color the ☆ As You Complete Your Daily Task

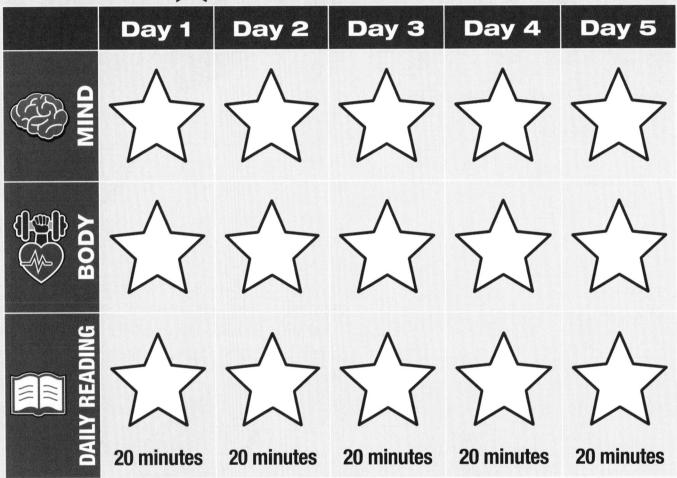

	Day 1	Day 2	Day 3	Day 4	Day 5
MIND	☆	☆	☆	☆	☆
BODY	☆	☆	☆	☆	☆
DAILY READING	☆	☆	☆	☆	☆
	20 minutes	20 minutes	20 minutes	20 minutes	20 minutes

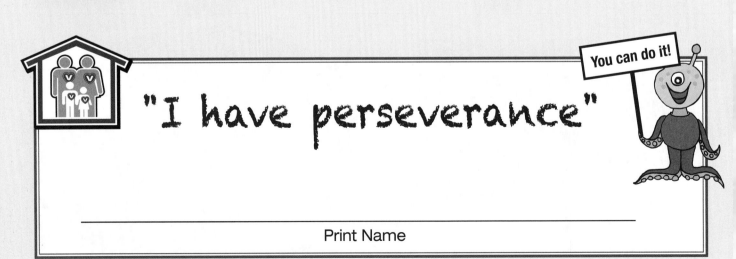

You can do it!

"I have perseverance"

_____

Print Name

Look at the word ending in each rocket.

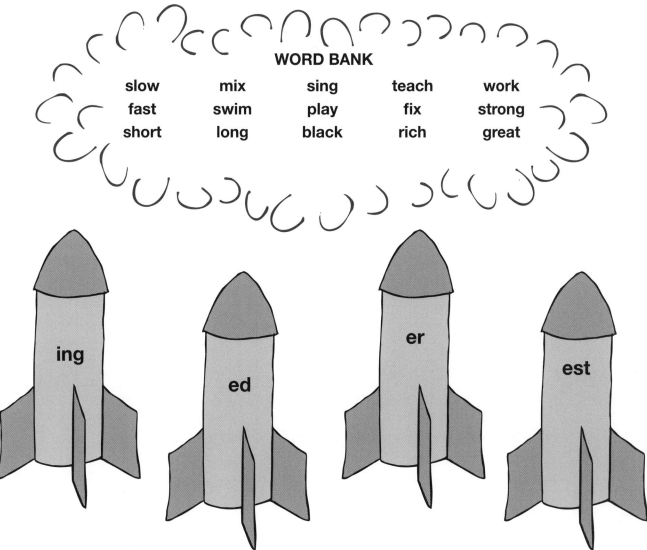

WORD BANK

slow	mix	sing	teach	work
fast	swim	play	fix	strong
short	long	black	rich	great

ing

ed

er

est

Use words from the word bank to make as many new words as you can .

teacher _____   _____   _____

teaching _____   _____   _____

_____   _____   _____

_____   _____   _____

_____   _____   _____

_____   _____   _____

Aerobic
Go to www.summerfitlearning.com for more Activities!

DAILY EXERCISE
Hula-Hoop
"Stretch Before You Play!"

Instruction
Goal = 20 times
without dropping

DAY 1

2

3

4

5

WEEK 9

Fabulous Fractions

Add or subtract these fractions with like denominators.

1. $\dfrac{2}{3} + \dfrac{5}{3} =$

2. $\dfrac{2}{4} + \dfrac{5}{4} =$

3. $\dfrac{3}{7} + \dfrac{2}{7} =$

4. $\dfrac{1}{5} + \dfrac{3}{5} =$

5. $\dfrac{1}{4} + \dfrac{2}{4} =$

6. $\dfrac{3}{4} - \dfrac{2}{4} =$

7. $\dfrac{3}{7} + \dfrac{4}{7} =$

8. $\dfrac{4}{5} + \dfrac{2}{5} =$

9. $\dfrac{6}{9} + \dfrac{3}{9} =$

Compare the fractions and fill in greater than (>), less than (<), or (=) to.

10. $\dfrac{1}{3}$ ____ $\dfrac{2}{3}$

11. $\dfrac{3}{4}$ ____ $\dfrac{1}{4}$

12. $\dfrac{1}{2}$ ____ $\dfrac{1}{4}$

13. $\dfrac{3}{4}$ ____ $\dfrac{1}{3}$

14. $\dfrac{1}{2}$ ____ $\dfrac{2}{4}$

15. $\dfrac{2}{4}$ ____ $\dfrac{3}{6}$

16. $\dfrac{1}{5}$ ____ $\dfrac{3}{5}$

17. $\dfrac{7}{10}$ ____ $\dfrac{8}{10}$

18. $\dfrac{6}{12}$ ____ $\dfrac{9}{12}$

Fill in the missing fractions on the number line.

19. $\dfrac{1}{9}$ $\dfrac{2}{9}$ ____ ____ ____ $\dfrac{6}{9}$ ____ $\dfrac{8}{9}$

A sentence is a group of words that express a complete thought, while a sentence fragment is a group of words that expresses an incomplete thought. Write S if the word is a sentence and F if it is a fragment. If the group of words is a fragment, rewrite on the line as a complete sentence.

Ex. The flowers in the garden. __F__ The flowers in the garden were planted by my mother.

1. The fire truck raced loudly down the street. _____ _____

2. Build nests in trees. _____ _____

3. My favorite food is pizza. _____ _____

4. The dog didn't like _____ _____

5. Mom baked a cake. _____ _____

6. I like to. _____ _____

7. Shoe salesman. _____ _____

8. I will ride the bus to school. _____ _____

9. I wish I. _____ _____

10. My friends and I had a sleepover. _____ _____

11. The camping trip. _____ _____

12. Clean your room! _____ _____

Write the article "a" or "an" before each word.

Ex. _An_ elephant   16. _____ eagle   20. _____ tree

13. _____ library   17. _____ ice cube   21. _____ egg

14. _____ igloo   18. _____ bat   22. _____ kite

15. _____ fly   19. _____ ape   23. _____ ant

Strength

Go to www.summerfitlearning.com for more Activities!

DAILY EXERCISE
Bottle curls
"Stretch Before You Play!"

Instruction
Repeat 5 times
with each arm

Be Healthy!
Turn off the TV and play outside.

WEEK 9

1

DAY 2

3

4

5

Wagon Wheel Multiplication

Use the number in the center of the wheel to multiply.

1.

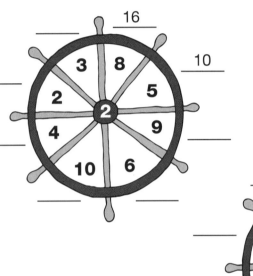

16

10

2.

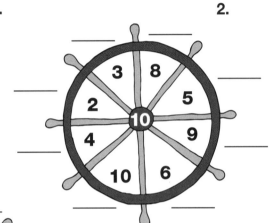

3.

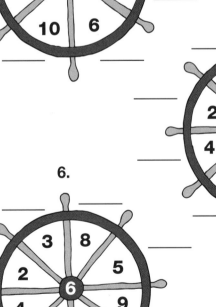

4.

5.

6.

© Summer Fit

An ecosystem is all the living and non-living things in a certain area and how they interact with each other. Living things in an ecosystem are the animals, plants, and bacteria in a community. Non-living things are things like rocks, soil, water, and air. There are six different ecosystems in the world: ocean, desert, tundra, forest , grasslands, and wetlands.

Look at the four examples of ecosystems. Write the name of each ecosystem described below.

Make an ecosystem diorama. Use a shoebox and decorate the inside to look like the landscape of your chosen ecosystem. Find or make pictures of the plants and animals that live and interact there and glue or hang them in your box. Write a paragraph or poem describing your ecosystem.

1

2

DAY 3

4

5

1. This ecosystem is very wet with an abundance of fish and turtles. Other living things include alligators, toads, snakes, cattails, crayfish, raccoons, waterweed, and muskrat.

This ecosystem is a _____.

2. This ecosystem is very dry with hot days and cool nights. Some of the plants and animals that live here are cactus, coyote, scorpion, roadrunner, rattlesnake, and tortoise.

The name of this ecosystem is a _____.

3. The plant and animal dwellers in this salty environment are diverse and include sharks, whales, dolphins, coral reef, starfish, jellyfish, swordfish, seaweed, kelp, and phytoplankton.

The name of this ecosystem is the _____.

4. This ecosystem is warm and wet and full of trees. It has an intricate group of plants and animals that depend on heavy rainfall. Some of the many plants and animals that live there include the gorilla, sloth, howler monkey, chameleon, jaguar, capybara, anaconda, ferns, orchid, and toucan.

The name of this ecosystem is_____.

WEEK 9

Aerobic

DAILY EXERCISE
Jump Rope
"Stretch Before You Play!"

Instruction
Goal = 3 minutes without stopping

Be Healthy!
Slow down when you eat!

1 **2** **DAY 3** **4** **5**

WEEK 9

Mixed Practice

Divide and check.

1. 3 | 8,031   2. 6 | 2,748

Multiply

3.	6,487	4.	4,320	5.	432	6.	621
	x 3		x 5		x 21		x 13

Continue each pattern using multiples of 10.

7. 10, 20, _____, _____, _____, 60	10. 800, 790, _____, _____, _____, 750
8. 150, 160, _____, _____, _____, 200	11. 1,210, 1,220, _____, _____, _____, 1,260
9. 340, 350, _____, _____, _____, 390	12. 5,670, 5,660, _____, _____, _____, 5,620

Solve quickly.

13. 8 x 4 = _____	16. 45 ÷ 5 = _____	19. 3 x 9 = _____	22. 36 ÷ 9 = _____
14. 6 x 6 = _____	17. 72 ÷ 9 = _____	20. 8 x 7 = _____	23. 9 x 4 = _____
15. 12 ÷ 2 = _____	18. 10 x 8= _____	21. 28 ÷ 4 = _____	24. 3 x 7 = _____

ABC
DE
GHI

Write about your greatest summer adventure. Be sure to include colorful adjectives and interesting facts. Use correct punctuation, spelling, and write in your best handwriting. Draw a picture to go with your story.

_____

_____

_____

_____

_____

_____

_____

_____

_____

_____

_____

_____

_____

_____

1

2

3

DAY 4

5

WEEK 9

Strength
Go to www.summerfitlearning.com for more Activities!

DAILY EXERCISE
Heel Raises
"Stretch Before You Play!"

Instruction
Repeat 8 times

Be Healthy!
Walk with your family before or after dinner.

Lines of Symmetry

Draw the lines of symmetry on each shape. Each shape could have none, one, or more than one line of symmetry.

Ex.

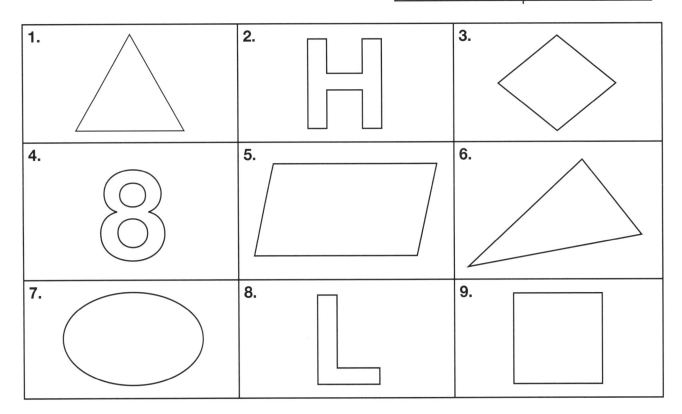

1.

2.

3.

4.

5.

6.

7.

8.

9.

Draw the other half of each object. The line of symmetry has been drawn for you.

10.

11.

12.

© Summer Fit

Spoungeworthy Photo by Phil Stefans

Perseverance means not giving up or giving in when things are difficult. It means you try again when you fail.

Bethany Hamilton Bethany Hamilton was sitting on her surfboard one sunny day in Hawaii, waiting for the next big wave. Suddenly a tiger shark attacked her and thirteen-year old Bethany lost one of her arms. Bethany survived and decided that she wanted to surf again. It wasn't easy because she had to overcome her fear of another shark attack and teach herself how to surf with only one arm. Little by little, she fought against the odds to succeed and was soon competing in and winning professional surfing competitions.

Bethany persevered and never gave up on her dreams. Rather than feel sorry for herself, she found a way to overcome her obstacles. Bethany decided that not only was she not going to give up on her dreams, but she wasn't going to let other kids give up on their dreams either. Bethany visited children in Thailand who had survived the Tsunami to help them get over their fears of getting in the water. She continues to travel around the world encouraging children with disabilities to follow their dreams no matter what. Bethany is proof that "where there is a will, there is a way."

Write a passage telling why Bethany Hamilton is a hero and how she has inspired you.

_____

_____

_____

_____

_____

Choose 1 or more activities to do with your family or friends. Color today's star when you are finished. Good job!

☐ Do a new art project that requires perseverance to complete.

☐ Try to learn something you have been afraid to try: a new sport, a musical instrument, sign language. Be patient and don't get discouraged as you learn the new skill.

☐ Learn about the history of the Olympics. How do Olympic athletes show perseverance. Choose an Olympic athlete to learn about and share with your family.

☐ Read a biography about a famous person who showed perseverance such as: Lewis and Clark, Susan B. Anthony, The Wright Brothers, or Louis Pasteur. What character traits did they have that helped them persevere?

Core Value Book List
Read More About Perseverance

The Big Wave
By Pearl S. Buck

The Cay
By Theodore Taylor

Julie of the Wolves
By Jean Craighead George

Reading Extension Activities at SummerFitLearning.com

Let's Talk About It
Encourage your child to try a variety of activities. Encourage them to keep trying even when they fail. Teach them that they don't always have to be the best at what they do but they do have to try their best at everything they do.

Play Time!
Choose a Game or Activity to Play for 60 minutes today!

YOU CHOOSE

Write down which game or activity you played today!

Be Healthy! Do something active everyday.

1

2

3

4

DAY 5

WEEK 9

WEEK 10

PARENT TIPS FOR WEEK 10

Skills of the Week

✔ E-mail book report
✔ Measurement
✔ 4th grade spelling words
✔ Reading a pictograph
✔ Landforms
✔ Calendar days
✔ Attitude of gratitude
✔ Fractions
✔ Factors
✔ Solve for x

Weekly Value Friendship

Lewis and Clark

Friendship is what comes from being friends. It is caring and sharing and being there for each other in good times and bad.

It is fun to have friends that we play with, go to the movies and share our time, but it also is a responsibility. Our friends are people that we trust, protect, respect and stand up for even when it is not easy. We care about our friends and our friends care about us.

GET FIT TIME!

Weekly Extension Activities at SummerFitLearning.com

Play 60 Every Day!

Run, jump, dance and have fun outside every day for 60 minutes!

Friendship In Action!

Color the star each day you show friendship through your own actions.

WEEK 10

HEALTHY MIND + HEALTHY BODY

Color the ★ As You Complete Your Daily Task

	Day 1	Day 2	Day 3	Day 4	Day 5
🧠 **MIND**	★	★	★	★	★
💪 **BODY**	★	★	★	★	★
📖 **DAILY READING**	★ 20 minutes	★ 20 minutes	★ 20 minutes	★ 20 minutes	★ 20 minutes

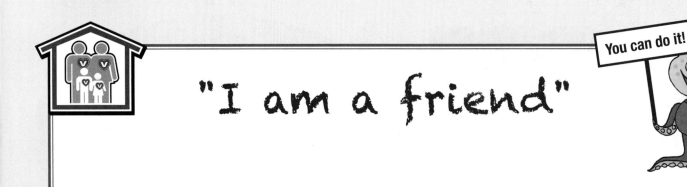

"I am a friend"

You can do it!

_____

Print Name

Choose a book that is non-fiction and is an appropriate reading level for you. Pick a book that you are interested in and write the title and author here.

Book Title: _____

Author: _____

Illustrator: (if there is one) _____

DAY 1

Read the book.

Now think of someone you think would enjoy this book too. This person can be a friend or relative. Think about the book you just read. What information could you share with your friend to peak their interest and make them want to read this book? What do you think they might want to know about the characters, plot, setting, writing style, etc.? Remember to organize your thoughts, give specific examples but don't give away the ending! Use persuasive writing to really peak your friend or relative's interest.

2

3

Print out what you would write your friend here. If your parents give their permission, send the email to your friend.

To: _____

4

From: _____

Dear_____, I just read a great book called _____

5

_____. I think you would really like it because _____

_____

_____.

Let me tell you about it. _____

_____

_____

_____

_____

_____

_____

_____

WEEK 10

Aerobic

Go to www.summerfitlearning.com for more Activities!

DAILY EXERCISE
Jogging for Fitness 15
"Stretch Before You Play!"

Instruction
Jog 15 minutes in place or outside

Be Healthy!
Eat more whole grains like pasta, bread and rice.

DAY 1

2 3 4 5

WEEK 10

Do You Know?

Fill in each blank with the appropriate measurement.

feet	inches	dozen	pounds	years	dollars
miles	yards	hour	minutes	gallon	ounces

1. Mom got a _____ donuts for my soccer team.

2. Dad is 6 _____ tall.

3. My dog weighs 40 _____.

4. I got a _____ of milk from the store.

5. I drank 16 _____ of soda.

6. The football field is 100 _____ long.

7. My grandpa is 65 _____ old.

8. The movie ticket cost five _____.

9. The next town is 45 _____ away.

10. The candy bar was 5 _____ long.

11. I read my book for 1 _____ last night.

12. I made my bed in 5 _____.

Read these spelling words to a parent or guardian. Then copy them, in cursive, in your best hand writing.

reindeer _____

column _____

weigh _____

neighbor _____

once _____

knowledge _____

alligator _____

handle _____

hymn _____

solemn _____

thumb _____

photograph _____

chalk _____

would _____

camera _____

entertain _____

Use words from the list above to answer the questions.

1. The children drew on the sidewalk with _____.

2. Many fairy tales begin with the words "_____ upon a time."

3. Another word for picture is _____.

4. To _____ something is to find out how heavy or light it is.

5. An upright structure that looks like a post is called a _____.

6. A word that means to amuse or keep interested is _____.

7. The funeral was a very _____ affair.

8. When the man lifted the heavy suitcase, the _____ broke.

9. To have no understanding or awareness of something is to have no _____ of it.

10. We brought our _____ Mr. Long dinner after he returned home from his surgery.

Strength
Go to www.summerfitlearning.com for more Activities!

DAILY EXERCISE
Lunges
"Stretch Before You Play!"

Instruction
Repeat 5 times with each leg

Be Healthy!
Learn a new joke today and tell it at dinner.

Pictograph

A pictograph uses pictures or symbols to show data. Use the pictograph to answer the questions below.

Mrs. Brown's 4th grade class voted on their favorite fruit.

Each face represents two votes. **= 2 votes**

Apples:

Bananas :

Watermelon:

Oranges:

Pineapple:

1. How many children like bananas most? _____

2. How many more children like watermelon than oranges? _____

3. What is the classes favorite fruit? _____

4. How many more children like apples than bananas? _____

5. What is the classes least favorite fruit? _____

6. How many children from Mrs. Brown's class voted? _____

The Earth is full of many different landforms. Draw a line from each picture to the name and description of its landform.

1.

2.

3.

4.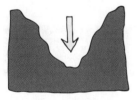

5.

6.

7.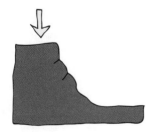

Island: land completely surrounded by water.

Plain: open, flat land.

Peninsula: land surrounded by water on three sides.

Valley: area of low land that is between mountains and hills.

Plateau: high, level, flat land

Volcano: mountain or hill made from melted rock.

Mountain: high land mass with steep sides.

Hill: slightly raised area of land.

Aerobic

Go to www.summerfitlearning.com for more Activities!

DAILY EXERCISE
Green Giant
"Stretch Before You Play!"

Instruction
Ask Mom for 15 minutes of yard work

Be Healthy!
Turn off the TV when you eat.

1

2

DAY 3

4

5

WEEK 10

Calendar Days

Write the abbreviation for each month's name. The number of days is in parenthesis.

1. January (31) _____   5. April (30) _____   9. July (31) _____

2. October (31) _____   6. February (28 or 29) _____   10. May (31) _____

3. August (31) _____   7. November (30) _____   11. March (31) _____

4. June (30) _____   8. September (30) _____   12. December (31) _____

Fill in the blanks.

13. 1 Year = _____ months.   16. 1 year has 52 _____.

14. 1 week has _____ days.

15. 1 year = _____ days unless it is a leap year then it has _____ days.

Sunday	Monday	Tuesday	Wednesday	Thursday	Friday	Saturday
		1	2	3	4	5
6	7	8	9	10	11	12
13	14	15	16	17	18	19
20	21	22	23	24	25	26
27	28					

17. What is the name of this month? _____

18. Circle all the Mondays. How many are there in this month? _____

19. According to this calendar is this a leap year? _____

20. If this was a leap year how many days would there be? _____

21. Circle one full week.

22. How many Sundays are in this month? _____

23. What day of the week is the 15th of this month? _____

An Attitude of Gratitude

Gratitude is the feeling of being thankful. It is when you thank someone for the good things they have done for you or given to you. Scientists have found that having a grateful attitude can help you have a happier, healthier life.

How many smaller words can you make from the letters in "GRATITUDE"?

_____   _____   _____

_____   _____   _____

_____   _____   _____

_____   _____   _____

Think of things you are grateful for. Make a list of at least 10 things:

1. _____
2. _____
3. _____
4. _____
5. _____
6. _____
7. _____
8. _____
9. _____
10. _____

There are many ways to say thank you. Unscramble these words to say thank you in another language. The beginning letter has been given to you.

French
11. ercim = m _____

Spanish
12. ragacsi = g _____

German
13. kande = d _____

- Each day write down or share at least three good things about your day.
- Remember to say thank you throughout the day.
- Write thank you cards immediately after receiving a gift.
- Tell your parents, family, and friends how much you appreciate them.

1 2 3 DAY 4 5 WEEK 10

Strength

Go to www.summerfitlearning.com for more Activities!

DAILY EXERCISE
Crunches
"Stretch Before You Play!"

Instruction
Repeat 5 times

1
2
3

DAY 4

5

WEEK 10

Mixed Practice

Add or subtract. Simplify.

1. 2/7 + 4/7 = _____

2. 6/9 – 3/9 = _____

3. 1/4 + 1/4 = _____

4. 4/15 + 6/15 = _____

5. 11/12 – 5/12 = _____

6. 3/10 + 4/10 = _____

7. 11/19 – 7/19 = _____

8. 12/20 + 4/20 = _____

9. 9/11- 7/11 = _____

Simplify each fraction. Ex. 2/4 = 1/2

10. 3/9 = _____

11. 2/6 = _____

12. 3/6 = _____

13. 4/8 = _____

14. 2/10 = _____

15. 5/15 = _____

The factors of 12 are 1,2,3,4,6, and 12:   (1 x 12 = 12   2 x 6 =12   3 x 4 =12)

What are the factors for each number?

16.   10: _____

17.   18: _____

18.   20: _____

19.   36: _____

Solve for x   Ex. 3 x = 9   x = 3

20. 5 x = 25   x = _____

21. 4 x = 16   x = _____

22. 10 x = 100   x = _____

23. 6 x = 24   x = _____

24. 12 x = 120   x = _____

25. 2 x = 50   x = _____

Friendship is what comes from being friends. It is caring and sharing and being there for each other in good times and bad.

Friends Through It All

Meriwether Lewis and William Clark were American explorers. They were friends over 200 years ago when the United States of America was new and young and only had 17 states. In 1803, President Thomas Jefferson wanted them to explore the unknown land beyond the Mississippi River. He asked them to begin trading with North American tribes, discover new plants and animals, chart a new passage to the West, and make maps of it all.

The pair and their crew traveled 7,689 miles over the course of 863 days. On the expedition, 122 new animals and 178 new plants were discovered.

The expedition of Lewis and Clark is a symbol of the American spirit of exploration. Lewis and Clark completed each others strengths and compensated for each others weaknesses. Together, they displayed some of the qualities of a great friendship: loyalty, trust, honor, honesty, and compassion.

1. Write a short story about an adventure that you would like to have with your best friend. Use a separate sheet of paper if you need to.

_____

_____

_____

_____

_____

2. Put these words in alphabetical order:

obstacles _____

adventure _____

kindness _____

Choose 1 or more activities to do with your family or friends. Color today's star when you are finished. Good job!

☐ Write an essay about friendship. Write about what being a friend means to you. What do true friends do? What shouldn't they do? How do friends behave and what happens when friends argue or disagree?

☐ Make a card to invite a friend over. When they arrive let them choose the activity you will do.

☐ Make some cookies for a new kid in the neighborhood, or go over and introduce yourself. Introduce them to the rest of the kids in the neighborhood.

Core Value Book List
Read More About Friendship

Charlotte's Web
By E.B. White

The Hundred Dresses
By Eleanor Estes-Louis Slobodkin

Because of Winn Dixie
By Kate DiCamillo

Reading Extension
Activities at
SummerFitLearning.com

Let's Talk About It

Discuss with your child the difference between having a good friend who they really know and having a lot that they don't really know. In today's world, social networks and web sites can add to the confusion about what friendship really means and the importance of having a few real friends.

Play Time!

Choose a Game or Activity to Play for 60 minutes today!

YOU CHOOSE

_____

Write down which game or activity you played today!

Be Healthy!
Tell someone "I love you."

EXTRAS
Fitness Index
Family Health and Wellness Tips
Summer Journal • Book Report
Answer Key • Certificate of Completion

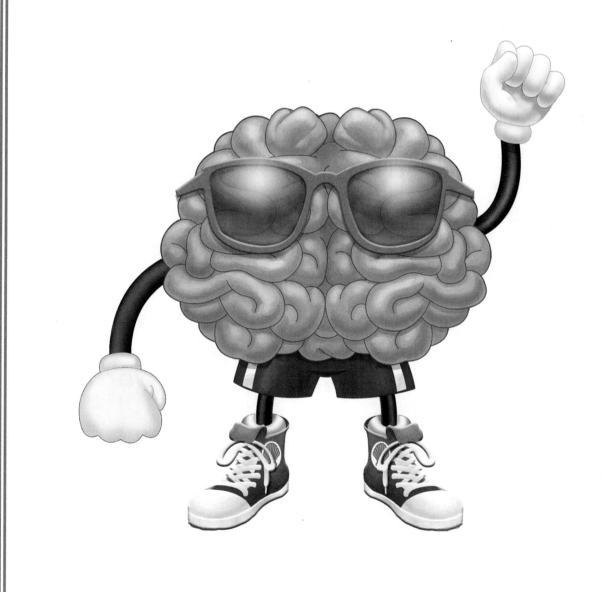

FITNESS INDEX

A healthy life is an active life. Kids need to be physically active for 60 minutes a day. Use the daily fitness activity to get moving. After 10 weeks of physical activity you have created a new and healthy lifestyle!

AEROBIC

Aerobic Exercise = Oxygen

The word "Aerobic" means "needing or giving oxygen." These *Summer Fit* exercises get the heart pumping and oxygen moving to help burn off sugars and calories!

STRENGTH

Strength Exercise = Muscle

Strength exercises help make muscles stronger. These *Summer Fit* exercises help build strong muscles to support doing fun activities around the house, school and outdoors!

SPORTS

Play Exercise = Sport Activity

Playing a different sport each week is an opportunity to use the *Summer Fit* oxygen and fitness exercises in a variety of ways. There are a lot of sports to choose from and remember that the most important thing about being *Summer Fit* is to have fun and play!

Warm Up Before Exercising

1 **Inchworm** – Put your hand on the ground in front of your feet. Walked out on the hands and then walk up on the feet. Do this 5 times.

2 **Knee Hug** – While you are slowly walking, pull your knee to your chest and hug. Do this 5 times on each leg.

3 **Toe Grab** – Toe Touch. Grab the toe behind your leg then touch the opposite toe with your opposite hand. Stand up and switch. Repeat 5 tines on each leg.

Warning:
Before starting any new exercise program you should consult your family physician. Even children can have medical conditions and at risk conditions that could limit the amount of physical activity they can do. So check with your doctor and then

Get Fit!

Aerobic Exercise = Oxygen

Aerobic exercises get you moving. When you move your heart pumps faster and more oxygen gets to your lungs. Movement helps burn off sugars and calories and gets you fit!

◆ **Jogging for Fitness 5**: Jog 5 minutes in place or outside:

◆ **Jogging for Fitness 10**: Jog 10 minutes in place or outside:

◆ **Jogging for Fitness 15:** Jog 15 minutes in place our outside:

◆ **Jumping Jacks:** Jump to a position with your legs spread wide and your hands touching overhead and then returning to a position with your feet together and arms at your sides. A more intense version is to bend down (over) and touch the floor in between each jump. **Goal = 20 Jumping Jacks**

◆ **Let's Jump:** Jump forward and back, jump side to side. Hop on one foot to another, moving side-to-side, alternating feet. Quicken your pace. Repeat. **Goal = 3 Sets of Jumps**

◆ **Let's Dance:** Step to your right with your right foot (putting your weight on your right foot). Step behind your right foot with your left foot (putting your weight on your left foot). Step again to the right with your right foot (weight on right) and touch your left foot next to your right (with your weight staying on the right foot). Repeat the above going left but switching to the other foot. **Goal = Dance for 5 minutes**

Do the Cha-cha
Step forward right, cha-cha
Step forward left, cha-cha
Repeat

Do the Cross over
Cross right over left, kick out right leg then backwards cha-cha-cha
Cross left over right, kick out left leg then backwards cha-cha-cha
Repeat

Do the Rope
Rope 1/4 to the left
1/4 facing the rear
1/4 turn left again
Rope to the front and step together with a clap.
Repeat
(When you "rope" hold one hand above your head and swing your arms in a circle like you have a rope above you).

◆ **Pass and Go/Get a Friend to Play this Game With You!:** This activity requires a second person. Ask a friend or someone from your family to play with you. The object of this activity is to pass a ball back and forth counting by 2's get to a 100 as fast as you can. Have a stopwatch handy. Set a time you want to beat and go! Increase your goal by setting a lower time. Repeat. **Goal = 100**

◆ **Step It Up/ Start Slow & Increase Your Speed:** This activity uses stairs if you have them. If you do, take three trips up and down the stairs. Raise your legs high like you are in a marching band. If you do not have stairs, do 20 step-ups on one step. **Goal = 20 steps**

◆ **Kangaroo Bounce:** Tape a shoelace to the floor in a straight line. Stand on one side of the string with both feet together. Jump forward over the string and then backward to land in your original place. Take a short break—and do it again. This time jump side-to-side over the shoelace. **Goal = 10 Times**

◆ **Hoops - Play to 11 by 1's:** A trash can makes a great indoor basketball goal— perfect for a quick game of one-on-one against yourself or a friend! Use a bottle-cap or crunched up ball of paper as your basketball. Twist, jump and make sure to use a few fakes to win the game! **Goal = 11**

◆ **Green Giant:** Mow the grass, weed the garden or pick up the yard.

◆ **Capture the Flag/ Get Your Family and Friends to Play:** Use scarves or old T-shirts for flags. Use a different color one for each team. Use chalk, cones, tape, or landmarks such as trees or sidewalks to divide your playing area into equal-sized territories for each team. Place one flag into each territory. It must be visible and once it is placed it cannot be moved. When the game begins, players cross into opposing teams' territories to grab their flags. When a player is in an opposing team's territory he/she can be captured by that team's players. If they tag him/her, he/she must run to the sideline and perform an exercise—for example, five jumping jacks or three push-ups. After they perform their exercise the player can go back to his/ her own team's territory and resume play. The game ends when one team successfully captures the flag(s) from the other team or teams and returns to their own territory with the opposing team's flag.

◆ **Happy Feet:** Use your feet every chance you get today. Walk to a friend's house, to the store, around the park or wherever it's safe to walk. **Goal = Get your parents to walk with you after dinner**

◆ **Let's Roll:** Put your lungs to work on your bike, skates or scooter. Don't forget to wear helmets and pads!

◆ **Speed:** Rest in between. See how fast you and your friends can run for one block. Time yourself and see if you can beat your original time. Repeat. **Goal = 2 blocks**

◆ **Hopscotch:** Toss a stone into the first square. The stone must land completely within the designated square without touching a line or bouncing out. Hop through the course, skipping the square with the marker in it. Single squares must be hopped on one foot. After hopping into "home" turn around and return through the course until you reach the square with their marker. Retrieve the marker and continue the course as stated without touching a line or stepping into a square with another player's marker. Upon successfully completing the sequence, toss the marker into square number two, and repeat the pattern. You cannot step on a line, miss a square, or lose balance. Complete one course for every numbered square.

◆ **Tag/ Get your family and friends to play:** A group of players (two or more) decide who is going to be "it", often using a counting-out game such as eeny, meeny, miny, moe. The player selected to be "it" chases the others, attempting to get close enough to tag them—touching them with a hand—while the others try to escape. A tag makes the tagged player "it" - in some variations, the previous "it" is no longer "it" and the game can continue indefinitely, while in others, both players remain "it" and the game ends when all players have become "it."

◆ **Hide-and-Seek/ Get your family and friends to play:** This is a game in which a number of players conceal themselves in the environment, to be found by one or more seekers. The game is played by one player (designated as being "it") counting to a predetermined number while the other players hide. After reaching the number, the player who is "it" tries to find the other players.
After the player designated as "it" finds another player, the found player must run to base, before s/he is tagged by "it." After the first player is caught they help the "it" seek out others. Last one found wins!

◆ **Hula-Hoop:** A hula-hoop is a toy hoop that is twirled around your waist, limbs or neck. Use your hips to twirl the hoop around your body as many times as you can. Set a time goal and work to reach it without letting the hoop drop to the ground. As you get better extend your goal! **Goal = 20 times without dropping**

◆ **Jump Rope:** is the primary tool used in the game of skipping where you jump over a rope swung so that it passes under your feet and over your head. Here are some different jumps that you can do:
Basic jump or easy jump: This is where both feet are slightly apart and jump at the same time over the rope. Beginners should master this technique first before moving onto more advanced techniques.
Alternate foot jump (speed step): This style consists of using alternate feet to jump off the ground. This technique can be used to effectively double the number of skips per minute as compared to the above technique. This step is used for speed events.
Criss-Cross: This method is similar to the basic jump with the only difference being that while jumping, the left hand goes to the right part of the body and vice versa for the right hand, with arms crossing in front of the body.
Side Swing: This is a basic technique where the rope passes the side of the skipper's body, without jumping it. Usually the skipper performs a basic jump after a side swing, or a criss-cross.

Strength Exercise = Muscle

Strength exercises make muscles stronger. When you build strong muscles you are able to lift more, run faster, and do fun activities around your house, school, and outdoors!

◆ **Knee lifts:** Stand with your feet flat on the floor. Start by lifting your right knee up 5 times, always bring both feet together between each interval then change legs. When you feel more confident, bounce while you bring your knee up and alternate between legs. **Goal = repeat 5 times with each leg**

◆ **Chin-ups:** These are difficult because they use weaker arm and back muscles. From a hanging position, pull yourself up with your torso straight. Use your arms, without twisting your back. Try to raise yourself until your chest is at or near the bar. Hold for one or two seconds then lower yourself down slowly. **Goal = 3 - 5 times**

◆ **Bottle curls:** Start with two bottles of laundry detergent (or any large bottle with a handle). Stand with your feet flat on the floor, shoulder width apart. Place both your hands in the same position on the handles of each bottle. With your back straight, slowly curl each bottle keeping your arm in the shape of an "L" until the bottle is raised to your shoulder. Only use bottles that you can lift easily and that do not cause you to stumble under their weight. **Goal = 5 times with each arm**

◆ **Heel Raises:** Heel raises strengthen the calf muscles. Stand with your feet a few inches apart, with your hands lightly resting on a counter or chair in front of you. Slowly raise your heels off the floor while keeping your knees straight. Hold for 5 seconds and then slowly lower your heels to the floor. Repeat. **Goal = 8 - 10 times**

◆ **Squats:** Start by placing your hands on your hips and stand with feet about shoulder width apart. Slowly move downward by bending your knees and keeping body straight by sticking out your butt. Squat as far down as you comfortably can, then slowly rise back up until you are standing straight. **Goal = 5 - 8 times**

◆ **Lunges:** Start by standing with your two feet shoulder length apart with your back straight and your arms by your sides. Simply lunge forward on one knee, count to two and then step back to your original position. After two counts lunge forward on your alternate foot. Always make sure that your front knee never goes beyond your toes. Make sure you keep your balance so you do not fall forward or to the side! **Goal = 5 - 7 times with each leg**

◆ **Push-ups (traditional or modified):** Practice getting your body into a straight position required for a pushup, by stiffening your body like a flat board. Get on the floor and rest on both forearms and toes, with your body stiff and straight off the floor. Keep your butt down without letting it droop towards the floor so it is straight with the rest of your body. When you are ready to start, take your forearms off the floor and place your hands where they were. Lower your body straight down until your chest almost touches the floor, and then push back up into your straight position. Keep your head up and look straight ahead. **Goal = 5 - 10 times**

To do a modified push up, get in your straight position and then rest on your knees. When you are ready to start, lower your body straight down while rocking forward on your knees to help take away some of your body weight. Push back up so you are in your original position. This is a great way to start learning push-ups and building your strength.

COACH JAME'S CORNER
Hey kids, Have fun moving and getting fit! More training videos at: SummerFitLearning.com

- **Crunches:** Start by sitting down on the floor, then bend your knees while moving your feet toward your butt. Keep your back and feet flat on the floor. Put your hands behind your head, or arms together in front of your body with your hands tucked under your chin. With your shoulders off the ground as the starting position, raise your head to your knees, using only core muscles. Then lower your body, keeping your shoulders slightly off the ground in the starting position. Try to keep your lower back on the floor and do not use your arms to pull yourself up. **Goal = 5 - 10 times**

- **Can Do:** Go to the kitchen and find two of the heaviest cans you can hold. Stand with your feet flat on the floor, with the cans in your hands and arms at your side. Lift the cans up to your chest, bending your arms at the elbows. Hold for two seconds, and then slowly lower your arms. **Goal = 3 - 5 times**

- **Sky Reach:** Choose a small object such as a ball, a book or even a piece of fruit. Make an "L" with your arm—with your upper arm at shoulder level and your forearm pointing toward the ceiling. Now extend your arm straight over your shoulder, pushing the object toward the sky. Return to the bent-arm position. **Goal = 3 - 5 times with each arm**

- **Bottle Lift:** Start with two bottles of laundry detergent (or any large bottle with a handle). Stand with your feet flat on the floor, shoulder width apart. Place the bottles on each side of your feet. Bend your knees, grab the bottles and stand up. **Goal = 5 - 10 times**

- **Chop n Squat:** Start with legs wide, bring your feet together, then out wide again, reach down and touch the ground, and pop up. **Goal = 7 - 10 times**

- **Side Step:** Lunge out to your right. Back leg straight, bend the right knee. Slide back and bend the left knee and straighten the right leg. Turn and face the opposite direction and repeat. **Goal = 5 times each direction**

- **Balance:** Balance on one foot. Foot extended low in front of you. Foot extended low in back of you. Foot extended low to the side. **Goal = hold each pose for 15 seconds**

- **Toe Taps:** Start by standing with your two feet shoulder length apart with your back straight and your arms by your sides. While jumping straight up, bring one toe forward to the front and tap while alternating to the opposite foot. Go back and forth between your left and right foot. Find a rhythm and be careful not to lose your balance! **Goal = 7 - 10 times with each Foot**

Summer Fit Tip

The more you workout and play with a partner the more they are likely to stick with it. Find a friend or someone in your family to exercise with everyday.

Marci and Courtney Crozier
Former Contestants of NBC's
The Biggest Loser

142   © Summer Fit

Exercise Activities for Kids

Find What You Like

Everybody has different abilities and interests, so take the time to figure out what activities and exercises you like. Try them all: soccer, dance, karate, basketball, and skating are only a few. After you have played a lot of different ones, go back and focus on the ones you like! Create your own ways to be active and combine different activities and sports to put your own twist on things. Talk with your parents or caregiver for ideas and have them help you find and do the activities that you like to do. Playing and exercising is a great way to help you become fit, but remember that the most important thing about playing is that you are having fun!

List of Exercise Activities

Home–Outdoor:

Walking
Ride Bicycle
Swimming
Walk Dog
Golf with whiffle balls outside
Neighborhood walks/Exploring (in a safe area)
Hula Hooping
Rollerskating/Rollerblading
Skateboarding
Jump rope
Climbing trees
Play in the back yard
Hopscotch
Stretching
Basketball
Yard work
Housecleaning

Home – Indoor:

Dancing
Exercise DVD
Yoga DVD
Home gym equipment
Stretch bands
Free weights
Stretching

With friends or family:

Red Rover
Chinese jump rope
Regular jump rope
Ring around the rosie
Tag/Freeze
Four score
Capture the flag
Dodgeball
Slip n Slide
Wallball
Tug of War
Stretching
Run through a sprinkler
Skipping
Family swim time
Bowling
Basketball
Hiking
Red light, Green light
Kick ball
Four Square
Tennis
Frisbee
Soccer
Jump Rope
Baseball

Turn off TV Go Outside - PLAY!
Public Service Announcement
Brought to you by Summer Fit

Chill out on Screen Time

Screen time is the amount of time spent watching TV, DVDs or going to the movies, playing video games, texting on the phone and using the computer. The more time you spend looking at a screen the less time you are outside riding your bike, walking, swimming or playing soccer with your friends. Try to spend no more than a couple hours a day in front of a screen for activities other than homework and get outside and play!

Health and Wellness Index

Healthy Family Recipes and Snacks

YOGURT PARFAITS: 01

Prep time: 15 minutes
Cook time: 0
Yield: 4 servings
Good for: all ages, limited kitchen, cooking with kids

Ingredients:
2 cups fresh fruit, at least 2 different kinds (can also be thawed fresh fruit)
1 cup low-fat plain or soy yogurt
4 TBSP 100% fruit spread
1 cup granola or dry cereal

YOGURT PARFAITS: 02

Directions:
Wash and cut fruit into small pieces
In a bowl, mix the yogurt and fruit spread together
Layer each of the four parfaits as follows:
Fruit
Yogurt
Granola (repeat)
Enjoy!
Kids can use a plastic knife to cut soft fruit
Kids can combine and layer ingredients

Tips:
A healthier dessert than ice cream
A healthy part of a quick breakfast

Jay Jacobs
Former Contestant
of NBC's
The Biggest Loser

It is important to teach children at a young age about the difference between a snack that is good for you versus a snack that is bad for you. It is equally important to teach your kids about moderation and how to eat until they are full, but not to overeat!

SMOOTHIES: 01

Prep time: 5 minutes
Cook time: 0
Yield: 2 servings
Good for: all ages,
limited kitchen, cooking with kids

Ingredients:
1 cup berries, fresh or frozen
4 ounces vanilla low fat yogurt
½ cup 100% apple juice
1 banana, cut into chunks
4 ice cubes

SMOOTHIES: 02

Directions:
Place apple juice, yogurt, berries, and banana in a blender. Cover and process until smooth

While the blender is running, drop ice cubes into the blender one at a time. Process until smooth

Pour and enjoy!
Kids can cut soft fruit and measure ingredients. They can also choose which foods to include.

Variation:
Add ½ cup of silken tofu or ½ cup of peanut butter for extra protein.

Crunchy, Fruity Cobbler: 01

Prep time: 5 minutes
Cook time: 5 minutes
Yield: 4 servings (1 cup=1 serving)
Good for: all ages of children

Ingredients:
1 (15 ounce) can of sliced peaches, drained*
1 (15 ounce) can of pear halves, drained*
1/4 tsp. of almond or vanilla extract
1/4 tsp. of ground cinnamon
3/4 cup of low-fat granola with rai
*Canned fruit should be packed in

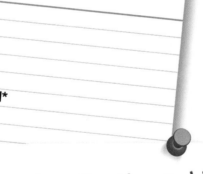

Crunchy, Fruity Cobbler: 02

Directions:
Combine the peaches, pears, extract and cinnamon in a microwave safe bowl. Stir well.
Sprinkle granola over the top.
Cover the bowl with a lid or plastic wrap, leaving a little opening for the steam to escape.
Microwave on high for 5 minutes.
Use potholders to remove the bowl from the microwave.
Let it cool a little, and then eat.

Kids in the Kitchen:
Kids can combine and stir the ingredients.

Health and Wellness Vocabulary

In order to teach your children the difference between healthy habits and unhealthy habits it is important to know and understand some of the basic terminology that you may hear in the media and from health experts.

Courtney Crozier
Former Contestant of NBC's *The Biggest Loser*

VOCABULARY

Calorie: A unit of measure of the amount of energy supplied by food.

Fat: It is one of the 3 nutrients (protein and carbohydrates are the other 2) that supplies calories to the body.

Protein: Is one of the building blocks of life. The body needs protein to repair and maintain itself. Every cell in the human body contains protein.

Carbohydrates: The main function is to provide energy for the body, especially the brain and nervous system.

Type 1 Diabetes: A disease characterized by high blood glucose (sugar) levels resulting in the destruction of the insulin-producing cells of the pancreas. This type of diabetes was previously called juvenile onset diabetes and insulin-dependent diabetes.

Type 2 Diabetes: A disease characterized by high blood glucose (sugar) levels due to the body's inability to use insulin normally, or to produce insulin. In the past this type of diabetes was called adult-onset diabetes and non-insulin dependent diabetes.

Sedentary lifestyle: A type of lifestyle with no or irregular physical activity. It pertains to a condition of inaction.

BMI: An index that correlates with total body fat content, and is an acceptable measure of body fatness in children and adults. It is calculated by dividing weight in kilograms by the square of height in meters. BMI is one of the leading indicators in determining obesity.

Obesity: Refers to a person's overall body weight and whether it's too high. Overweight is having extra body weight from muscle, bone, fat and/or water. Obesity is having a high amount of extra body fat.

Fiber: This is not an essential nutrient, but it performs several vital functions. A natural laxative, it keeps traffic moving through the intestinal tract and may lower the concentration of cholesterol in the blood.

Nutrient dense foods: Foods that contain relatively high amounts of nutrients compared to their caloric value.

Screen time: The amount of time a person participates in watching or playing something on a screen. The screen could be a television, computer, computer games, and a variety of electronics that interact with people utilizing a screen of various sizes. The American Academy of Pediatrics recommends no screen time before age 2 and no more that 1-2 hours of screen time for children over age 2.

Food label: Information listed inside a square box on prepared food packaging that shows the nutritional value of a product one consumes. It also gives the value shown as a percentage of the daily nutritional values that the Food and Drug Administration (FDA) recommend for a healthy diet.

Serving size: This term is used by the United States Department of Agriculture (USDA) to measure amounts of food. It is a tool for healthy eating.

Fat: is a source of energy. Fats perform many important functions in the body. There are healthy fats and unhealthy fats.

Monounsaturated and polyunsaturated oils: These contain some fatty acids that are HEALTHY. They do not increase the bad cholesterol in the body. Some of the foods in this category include fish, nuts and avocados.

Saturated fat: This "solid" fat increases bad cholesterol which can lead to it building up in the arteries and cause disease, more specifically, heart disease.

Trans fat: This fat is mostly found in processed foods and it contains unhealthy oils (partially hydrogenated). This type of fat has been shown to increase the bad cholesterol in the body and lower the good cholesterol.

Preadolescent: generally is defined as ages 9-11 years of age for girls and 10-12 years for boys.

Middle childhood: generally defines children between the ages of 5 to 10 years of age.

"School age": is another word for middle childhood.

"Tween": a relatively new term for a child between middle childhood and adolescence.

Health and Wellness Child Nutrition

1. Preadolescent ("tweens") and school age children's growth continues at a steady, slow rate until the growth spurt they will experience in adolescence. Children of this age continue to have growth spurts that usually coincide with increased appetite. Parents should not be overly concerned about the variability and intake of their school-age children.
2. The importance of family mealtimes cannot be stressed enough. There is a positive relationship between families who eat together and the overall quality of a child's diet.
3. Continue to have your child's BMI-for-age percentile monitored to screen for over and underweight.
4. In this age group the choices a child makes about his or her food intake are becoming more and more influenced by their peers, the media, coaches, and teachers. These outside influences steadily increase as a child ages and becomes more independent.
5. School plays a key role in promoting healthy nutrition and physical activity, so try to participate in healthy, school-related activities with your child, such as walk to school days and volunteering in the school's garden club.
6. Limited physical activity, along with sedentary activities are major contributing factors to the sharp increase of childhood obesity.
7. Soft drink or soda consumption, which tends to increase as a child ages, is associated with increased empty caloric intake and an overall poorer diet. These soft drinks also are a major contributor to dental caries. Diet sodas have no nutrient value, though they are not high in calories.
8. Complications from overweight and obesity in childhood and adolescence are steadily rising. This is including type 2 diabetes (usually adult onset diabetes) and high cholesterol levels.
9. Those children in the age ranges of middle childhood and preadolescence are strongly encouraged to eat a VARIETY of foods and increase physical activity to 60 minutes every day. Parents should set a good example by being physically active themselves and joining their children in physical activity.
10. Parents with healthy eating behaviors and are physically active on a regular basis are excellent role models for their children.

Healthy Websites

www.myplate.gov

www.readyseteat.com

www.nourishinteractive.com

www.cdph.ca.gov/programs/wicworks

www.cdc.gov
(food safety practices, childhood diabetes and obesity)

www.who.int

www.championsforchange.net

www.nlm.nih.gov/medlineplus

Healthly Lifestyles Start at Home

Staying active and healthy is important because it will have a positive impact on every aspect of your life.

Jay and Jen Jacobs
Former Contestants of NBC's
The Biggest Loser

1 **Lead by example:** Your children will do what they see you do. Eat your fruits and vegetables, go for walks and read a book instead of watching television. Your child will see and naturally engage in these activities themselves.

2 **Limit Screen Time:** The American Academy of Pediatrics recommends no screen time before age 2 and no more that 1-2 hours of screen time for children over age 2. Instead of limiting screen time for just them, try regulating it as a household. Keep a log of technology time, note "Screen Free Zones" like the bedroom and try shutting off all technology at least 1 day a week.

3 **Talk at the Table:** Sitting down with the family for dinner gives everybody an opportunity to reconnect and share experiences with each other. Limit distractions by not taking phone calls during dinner and turning the television off.

4 **Drink More Water (and milk):** Soda and other packaged drinks are expensive and contain a lot of sugar and calories. Set an example by drinking water throughout the day and encourage your children to drink water or milk when they are thirsty. These are natural thirst quenchers that provide the mineral and nutrients young (and old) bodies really need.

5 **Portion Control:** There is nothing wrong with enjoying food, but try to eat less. Use smaller plates so food is not wasted and teach your children to tell the difference between being satisfied and overeating.

6 **Make Time For Family Play:** Instead of sitting down to watch TV together plan an activity as a family. Go for a walk or bike ride, work on the yard together, visit the neighbor as a family. It's a great way to reduce technology, but more importantly a great opportunity to enjoy time together as a family.

SUMMER JOURNAL

Write about your
family vacation.

SUMMER JOURNAL

Write about your favorite
outdoor summer activity
Ex: Camping, swimming or biking.

SUMMER JOURNAL

Write about your
best summer day.

SUMMER JOURNAL

Write about one of your favorite things to do at home during the summer.

SUMMER JOURNAL

Write about your best friend

Summer Fit Book Report
Third to Fourth Grade

Title: _____

Author: _____

Genre (scary, mystery, adventure, biography): _____

Describe the setting: _____

_____

Protagonist (Main Character): _____

_____

Antagonist (Person who is against the protagonist): _____

_____

Summary of the plot: _____

_____

_____

_____

What was your impression of the book? What did you like and dislike about the book?

_____

_____

Would you recommend this book to a freind? Why or why not?

_____

_____

_____

Pretest Answers:

1. 5,215
2. a. 4,436 b. 9,812
3. 2,000
4. 114,134,364,411.
5. 2,8,7,6.
6. a. 150 b. 80 c. 650
7. a. 600 b. 100 c. 800
8. 3,000 + 900 + 70 + 4
9. a. 549 b. 7,822 c. 2,559 d. 406
10. 14,5,8,21,12,9,18,35,32,24,18, 56,45,56,48,22,54,36,27,16,36,15, 64,42,12.
11. a. 1,304 b. 9,380 c. 61,074 d. 16,328
12. a. 5 b. 4 c. 6 d. 6 e. 6 f. 9 g. 10 h. 6
13. a. 15 r. 2 b. 61 c. 961 d. 347
14. a. 1/2 colored b. 1/4 colored c. 1/3 colored d. 2/4 colored.
15. small, gray, tile, tiny.
16. a. Ouch! That hurt! b. What time does the movie start? c. I am so happy to be on summer vacation.
17. a. afraid b. smart c. complete (answers may vary.
18. a. below b. light c. hot (answers may vary.
19. Aunt Megan, Seattle, Washington.
20. John, Joseph,
21. factory, freedom, giant, group, harbor.
22. a. pair b. read
23. a. I'll b. you're c. it's
24. a. wolves b. babies c. girls
25. a. er b. est c. ing
26. c
27. as-tro-naut
28. noon, spoon, raccoon, balloon (answers vary.
29. a. am b. does c. an d. there

p. 19: 1. not very often   2. feeling bad 3. enjoys it   4. teasing me 5. understand   6. taking a risk 7. pouring rain   8. wiggling around 9. go to bed   10. day dreaming 11. go ahead and eat   12. don't know what to say   13. easy

p. 20: 1. 60 2. 170 3. 290 4. 360 5. 100 6. 390 7. 130 8. 800 9. 100 10. 200 11. 600 12. 4,000 13. 5,200 14. 8,400 15. 2,000 16. 8,000 17. 5,000 18. 1,000 19. 2,000 20. 5,000 21. 7,000 22. 10,000 23. 8,000

p. 21: 1. arachnid 2. eight legs, two body parts, many eyes 3. vibrations they feel with tiny hairs 4. molt 5. spinnerets 6. head, abdomen

p. 22: Prime Numbers (2,3,5,7,11,13, 17,19,23,29,31,37,41,43,47) Square around number one; 8, 24, 12, 16, 45

p. 23: 1. dry 2. asleep 3. sad 4. go 5. float 6. white 7. loud 8. couch 9. huge 10. smart 11. fair 12. happy 13. yelled

p. 24: 1. 1 2. 3 3. 2 4. 2 5. 3 6. 1 7. 2 8. 1 9. 3 10. 22 11. 5 12. 4

● Right
● Obtuse
● Acute

p. 25: Answers Vary 1. beautiful, strong, honest 2. rotten, smelly 3. creative, studios, trustworthy 4. hot, lazy, busy 5. funny, kind, honest 6. sweet, juicy, delicious 7. delicious, chocolate, 8th 8. soft, furry, tiny 9. striped, new, blue

p. 26: Row 1: (3) 3, 12, 18, 9, 15, 27, 24, 21, 6, 30 Row 2: (6) 6, 24, 36, 18, 30, 54, 48, 42, 12, 60 Row 3: (9) 9, 36, 54, 27, 45, 81, 72, 63, 18, 90 Row 4: (4) 4, 16, 24, 12, 20, 36, 32, 28, 8, 40 Row 5: (1): 1, 4, 6, 3, 5, 9, 8, 7, 2, 10 Row 6: (5): 5, 20, 30, 15, 25, 45, 40, 35, 10, 50 Row 7: (7): 7, 28, 42, 21, 35, 63, 56, 49, 14, 70 Row 8: (2): 2, 8, 12, 6, 10, 18, 16, 14, 4, 20 Row 9: (10): 10, 40, 60, 30, 50, 90, 80, 70, 20, 100 Row 10: (8): 8, 32, 48, 24, 40, 72, 64, 56, 16, 80 11) 138 12) 42

p. 27: 1. log cabin 2. read 3. honesty 4. president 5. slavery

p. 31: 1. geese 2. mice 3. boxes 4. boys 5. dogs 6. babies 7. men 8. puppies 9. tables 10. calves 11. coats 12. fish 13. watches 14. wolves 15. leaves 16. ladies 17. bunnies 18. monkeys 19. dishes 20. letters

p. 32: 1. yes 2. no 3. no 4. no 5. yes 6. no

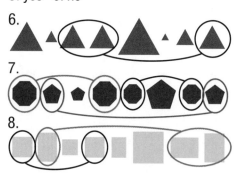

p. 33: 1. will 2. am 3. were 4. are 5. is 6. was 7. my, her 8. her, hers 9. our 10. your 11. their 12. my, her 13. our, its 14. his, his 15. her, hers 16. mine, yours

p. 34: 1. VI 2. VIII 3. II 4. IV 5. X 6. V 7. XIII 8. IX 9. 20, 17, 19, 27, 100, 4, 62, 40, 23 10. XXXVI, LV, XIV, XXIX, XL, XXI 11. II, IV, V, VII, VIII, IX, XI, XII

p. 35: 1. Prefix = re; Root Word = wash; wash again 2. Prefix = ex; Root Word = change; change from 3. Prefix = re; Root Word = build; build again 4. Prefix = de; Root Word = crease; make less 5. Prefix = re; Root Word = teach; teach again 6. Prefix = de; Root Word = tour; tour away 7. Prefix = pre; Root Word = school; before kindergarten 8. Prefix = re; Root Word = do; do again 9. Prefix = pre; Root Word = pay; pay before 10. Prefix = ex; Root Word = claim; speak out 11. Answers Vary 12. Answers Vary 13. Answers Vary

p. 36: 1. 925 2. 7,416 3. 375
4. 214 5. Three hundred twenty
6. One thousand eight hundred fifty-two 7. Five thousand two hundred forty-eight 8. Three thousand nine hundred eighty 9. 500 + 90 + 8
10. 4,000 + 300 + 60 +7 11. 6,000 + 700 + 80 + 1 12. 8,000 + 100 + 3
13. 1,743 14. 3,529 15. 9,265
16. 5,982 17. 300 18. 600 19. 65
20. 7,000 21. 85 22. 200

p. 37: 1. hummingbird 2. woodpecker
3. chameleon 4. penguin 5. capybara
6. raccoon

Extra credit: South America; North America; hum-ing-bird; wood-peck-er; cap-y-bar-a

p. 38: 1. 3/8; 2. 2/3; 3. 1/2;
4. 3/10; 5. 5/9; 6. 5/6; 7. = 8. <
9-11 Answers Shaded

p. 39: 1-6 Answers Vary

p. 43: 1. a child's imagination 2. dark brown 3. leaves, castles, boats
4. far away 5. more/ashore
6. answers vary

p. 44: 1. 12,15,30,27,6,18,24,3,21,9
2. 36,12,30,24,54,18,42,60,48,6
3. 20,12,4,40,24,8,28,16,36,32
4. 24,80,48,64,16,32,8,56,72,40
5. 50,5,30,10,20,40,35,15,45,25
6. 21,14,56,63,35,49,28,42,7,70

p. 45: 1. thing 2. thing 3. place
4. person 5. thing 6. place 7. person
8. person 9. place 10. thing
11. place 12. person 13. person
14. thing 15. place 16. movie
17. month 18. state 19. holiday
20. store 21. street 22. dog
23. boy 24 – 31. answers vary

p. 46: 1. 143 2. 698 3. 549 4. 534
5. 251 6. 552 7. 211 8. 289
9. 2 10. 40 11. 7 12. 48 13. 5

14. 10 15. 4 16. 36 17. 3 18. 4
19. 16   20. 40,35,30,25,20,15,10,5
21. 26,28,30,32,34,36,38,40
22. 18,21,24,27,30,33,36,39
23. 150,160,170,180,190,200,210,220

p. 47: 1. verbs; run, whisper, swim, hop, sing, crawl, eat, jump, drink, bark
2. swim, swam, will swim 3. play, played, will play 4. sing, sang, will sing 5. draw, drew, will draw

p. 48: 1. 120 2. 97 3. 148 4. 80
5. 24 6. 20 7. 12 8. 20 9. 22
10. 19 11. 50 12. 100 13. 299,301
14. 18 15. 349 16. 1277 17. 4,999, 5,001 18. 9,000 19. 1,000
20. 6:45 21. 2:25 22. 10:05

p. 49: 1. tail 2. week 3. too 4. read
5. know 6. write 7. where 8. flour
9. due 10. peak 11. male 12. leak

p. 50: 1. 16cm 2. 20cm 3. 22cm
4. 36cm 5. 34cm 6. 15cm 7. 6cm
8. 44cm 9. 52cm 10. each side is 2cm

p. 51: 1. she did what she said
2. helped others while risking her life
3. kept her word 4. helped the slaves
5-6. answers vary

p. 55: 1. out 2. water 3. woman
4. school 5. sad 6. vegetable
7. night 8. leg 9. hear 10. cold
11. book 12. sheep

p. 56: 1. $1.96 2. $1.60 3. $1.89
4. $8.10 5. $ .35 6. $5.95
7. answers vary
8. $1.25, $6.70, $10.50, $15.00, $59.75, $25.50, $.09, $12.46, $100.65

p. 57: 1. payment 2. washable
3. frighten 4. breakable 5. invention
6. improvement 7. soften 8. direction
9. collected 10. careful 11. fearless
12. louder 13. fastest 14. walking
15. gladness 16. neater
17. thoughtless 18. cheated

19. sleeping   20. safely
21. root=happy;pre=un;suffix=ness
22. root=pack;pre=un;suffix=ing
23. root=frost;pre=de;suffix=ed
24. root=paint;pre=re;suffix=ed
25. root=correct;pre=in;suffix=ly
26. root=claim;pre=ex;suffix=ed
27. root=perfect;pre=im;suffix=ly
28. root=comfort;pre=un;suffix=able

p. 58: 1. 1,560 2. 5,650 3. 5,650
4. 506 5. 56 6. 600 7. 60
8. 6,000 9. 6 10. 50 11. 500
12. 5 13. 5,000 14. 20 15. 200
16. 2 17. 2,000
18. 89,129,568,652,1,067

p. 59: 1. 200 2. calcium
3. brain, heart, lungs 4. bone marrow
5. blood cells 6. femur 7. 16

p. 60: 1. 8:16 2. 8:50 3. 11:25
4. 3:10 5. 6:40 6. 12:25 7. 9:35
8. 12:15 9. eighteen minutes after three 10. five minutes before three
11. twenty nine minutes after seven
12. twenty five minutes before ten

p. 61: 1. hard 2. dark 3. whisper
4. walk 5. laugh 6. careful 7. clean
8. happy 9. near 10. low 11. over
12. hot 13. in 14. down 15. stop
16. awake 17. lose

p. 62: 1. 8,001 2. 6,462 3. 12,247
4. 2,252 5. 2,402 6. 4,420 7. 3,522
8. 2,192 9. 77 10. 140 11. 99
12. 175 13. 530 14. 109 15. 258
16. 617 17. 667 18. 209 19. 589
20. 1,034 21. 178 22. 433
23. 9,790 24. 1,664

p. 63: 1. F 2. T 3. F 4. T 5. T . F

p. 67: 1. Joseph had a sleepover with his friends Brendan, Jacob, and Sam. 2. I am going to visit my friend Isabella in San Diego, California. 3. Ouch! A mosquito bit me on the leg!
4. "Christmas is my favorite holiday,"

said Beth. 5. Mom packed us a delicious picnic lunch of sandwiches, chips, carrot sticks, and cookies. 6. Grandma's favorite hobby is water skiing on Bear Lake. 7. Jonathan and Noah went to the circus on Saturday. 8. Amy watered the plants and pulled the weeds in the garden. 9. Ants use their antennae to smell, touch, and find food.

p. 68: Draw 25 triangles, five in each row and divide 25 by 5.
1. 8 2. 6 3. 4 4. 3 5. 7 6. 9
7. 4 8. 5 9. 4 10. 5 r2 11. 61
12. 9 r6 13. 32 14. 23 r3 15. 159
16. 218 17. 844

p. 69: 1. Idaho 2. Olympia 3. Utah
4. Arizona 5. Canada 6. California
7. Pacific Ocean 8. Salem
9. California, Nevada, Utah, Colorado, New Mexico 10. New Mexico

p. 70: Heart

p. 71: 1. 2,2,2 2. 5,5,2 3. 1,1,1,
4. 4,3,3 5. 4,4,4, 6. 2,2,2 7. 3,3,3
8. 2,2,2 9. 4,4,4
(circle dictionary) 10. ba-na-na
11. be-cause 12. flow-ers
13. neigh-bor-ly 14. wood-peck-er
15. sweat-er 16. book-case
17. re-al-ize 18. hap-pi-ness

p. 72: 1. 4,914 2. 1,377 3. 6,311
4. 42,068 5. 100,845 6. 2,592
7. 344,760 8. 735 9. 12 10. 24
11. 7 12. 3 13. 2 14. 1 15. 60
16. 36 17. 2

p. 73: 1. sun 2. precipitation
3. condensation 4. water

p. 74: 1. equilateral 2. scalene
3. right 4. isosceles 5. right
6. scalene 7. equilateral 8. right

p. 75: 1. charity work 2. look up in dictionary

p. 79: 1. 3 kinds of rocks 2. chapter 5
3. chapter 6 4. p. 20 5. p. 12
6. chapter 4 7. he'll 8. can't
9. you're 10. I'm 11. they've
12. she's 13. hasn't 14. we'll
15. we're 16. isn't 17. they're
18. won't

p. 80: 1. 0.8 2. .7 3. .75 4. .9
5. .5 6. .3 7. .10 8. .90 9. 1/4
10. 6/10 11. 2/10 12. 5/10
13. 4/10 14. 75/100 15. 4/10
16. 9/10 17. 15/100 18. 35/100
19. 1/5 20. 1/2 21. 2/3 22. 4/5
23. 1/10 24. 4/7

p. 81: 1. T 2. T 3. F; Bats like to live in colonies 4. T 5. F; Bats are not birds. 6. T 7. F; Bats use sonar called echolocation 8. F; Most bats eat insects 9. T

p. 82: 1. 6 2. 8 3. 9 4. 3 5. 12
6. 10 7. 9 8. 4 9. 86,680,806,860
10. 154,456,540,654
11. 70,78,87,107
12. 105,450,505,555
13. 59,56,53,50,47
14. 28,35,42,49,56
15. 74,72,70,68,66
16. 130,135,140,145,150
17. 170,160,150,140,130
18. 62,64,66,68,70
19. 132, 3,370, 350, 124
20. 676, 5,334, 445, 1,707
21. 689, 98, 460, 251
22. 2,460, 1,793, 2,890, 230

p. 83: 1. patiently;adverb
2. loudly;adverb 3. brightly;adverb
4. tirelessly;adverb 5. curly;adjective
6. smelly;adjective 7. bravely;adverb
8. gently;adverb 9. friendly;adjective
10. quickly;adverb
11. beautiful;ballerina 12. shy;boy
13. pretty;bouquet 14. fluffy;kitten
15. marching;band
16. patient; librarian, large:group
17-20. Answers Vary

p. 84: 1. > 2. < 3. < 4. < 5. <
6. > 7. < 8. = 9. < 10. < 11. <
12. = 13. > 14. = 15. > 16. =
17. feet 18. feet 19. yards
20. miles 21. inches 22. centimeters
23. quart 24. inch 25. mile
26. week 27. minute 28. pound
29. yard 30. dime

p 85: 1. big spider; built a web under the porch 2. Amanda and Rachel; visited the Doll and Toy Museum
3. space alien; landed his ship in the field 4. Joe and his brother; played in the chest tournament 5. children; played in the sandbox 6. moon and stars; shone brightly in the sky
7. horse; galloped across the field
8. We; rode the bus to the zoo 9-10. Answers Vary

p 86: 1. 100 F 2. 10 C 3. 40 F
4. 212 5. 0 6. thermometer 7. color in thermometer

p 87: Answers Vary

p. 91: Answers Vary

p. 92: 1. $1.00 2. $2.00 3. $2.00
4. $20.00 5. $13.00 6. $6.00
7. $9.00 8. $13.00 9. $16.00
10. $8.00 11. $.88 12. $2.15
13. $41.50 14. $48.75 15. $38.58
16. $102.14 17. $167.00 18. $122.70

p. 93: 1. house 2. button 3. cats and dogs 4. rock 5. baby 6. pancake
7. glove 8. hyena 9. old shoe
10-12. Answers Vary

p. 94: 1. 4 2. 5 3. 6 4. 5 5. 6
6. $.50 7. $.25 8. 8 9. 8 10. 20
11. 41 12. 13 13. 14

p. 95: 1-8. Check your work with a map of the United States of America

p. 96: 1. 0-9-8-7   2. 1-2-7-6
3. 5-8-2-0   4. 0-6-9-4
5. 9-0-4-1   6. 8-3-4-9
(7-10)- 6 + 6 + 6 ; 3+3+3+3+3+3; 6 x 3; 3 x 6
(11-14) 8 + 8 + 8 + 8 ; 4 + 4 + 4 + 4 + 4 + 4 + 4; 4 x 8; 8 x 4
15. 8:15   16. 7:50

p. 97: 1. is   2. are   3. were   4. was
5. am   6. am   7. are   8. were   9. are
10. is

p. 98: 1. parallel   2. perpendicular
3. intersecting   4. intersecting
5. parallel   6. perpendicular   7. one
8. two   9. one   10. one   11. one
12. two

p. 99: 1. worthless   2. weakness
3. lose   4. arrogant   5. war   6. help
7. Answers Vary

p. 103: 1. 90%   2. Arctic, Southern, Indian, Atlantic, Pacific   3. Explores and studies the ocean and all that it contains.   A vessel capable of operating or remaining under water

p. 104: 1. March   2. April   3. 60
4. 90   5. 10,15,25,50,60,65,90,95,100
6. 90

p. 105: 1. mowed   2. ate   3. toasted
4. chirped   5. boils   6. playing
7. cooking   8. making   9. will skate
10. will catch   11. will hatch
12. will practice

p. 106: 1. 8:45; 10:30; 15 minutes
2. 3:35; 2:45; 40 minutes
3. 11:35; 12:55; 40 minutes
4. $48.00   5. $3.13   6. 8 cookies

p. 107: firm, fish, fishhook, first, fisherman   1. 4,3,5,2,1
2. 1,2,3,4,5   3. 5,4,3,1,2   4. 1,4,2,5,3

p. 108: 1. $3.10   2. $1.90   3. $6.50
4. $3.50   5. no, $.35   6. salad
7. fries   8. $7.20

p. 109: Answers Vary

p. 110: 1. 12   2. 35   3. 72   4. 48
5. 50   6. 32

p. 111: 1. Canada   2. cancer
3. research   4. money   5. Hope
6. amputate; Cut off (a limb., typically by surgical operation)

p. 115: Faster, fastest, swimmer, swimming, longer, longest, etc. Continue making as many new words as you can.

p. 116: 1. 2 1/3   2. 7/4 = 1 3/4
3. 5/7   4. 4/5   5. 3/4   6. 1/4
7. 7/7 = 1   8. 6/5 = 1 1/5
9. 9/9 = 1   10. <   11. >   12. >
13. >   14. =   15. =   16. <   17. <
18. <   19. 3/9, 4/9, 5/9, 7/9

p. 117: 1. S   2. F; Birds build nests in trees.   3. S   4. F; The dog didn't like being left in the rain.   5. S
6. F; I liked to ride my bike.
7. F; My uncle is a shoe salesman.
8. S   9. F; I wish I could go to the moon.   10. S   11. F; The camping trip was fun.   12. S   13. a   14. an   15. a
16. an   17. an   18. a   19. an   20. a
21. an   22. a   23. an

p. 118: Use calculator to check your answers.

p. 119: 1. swamp   2. desert   3. ocean
4. forest

p. 120: 1. 2,677   2. 458   3. 19,461
4. 21,600   5. 9,072   6. 8,073
7. 30,40,50   8. 170, 180, 190
9. 360, 370, 380   10. 780, 770, 760
11. 1,230, 1,240, 1250
12. 5,650, 5,640, 5,630   13. 32
14. 36   15. 6   16. 9   17. 8   18. 80
19. 27   20. 56   21. 7   22. 4   23. 36
24. 21

p. 121: Answers Vary

p. 122: 1. one   2. two   3. two   4. two
5. two   6. none   7. two   8. none
9. four 10-12. draw the other half

p. 123: Answers Vary

p. 127: Answers Vary

p. 128: 1. dozen   2. feet   3. pounds
4. gallon   5. ounces   6. yards
7. years   8. dollars   9. miles
10. inches   11. hour   12. minutes

p. 129: 1. chalk   2. once
3. photograph   4. weigh   5. column
6. entertain   7. solemn   8. handle
9. knowledge   10. neighbor

p. 130: 1. 8   2. 2   3. apples   4. 4
5. pineapple   6. 32

p. 131: 1. peninsula   2. plain
3. volcano   4. valley   5. mountain
6. island   7. plateau

p. 132: 1. Jan.   2. Oct.   3. Aug.
4. June   5. Apr.   6. Feb.   7. Nov.
8. Sept.   9. July   10. May   11. Mar.
12. Dec.   13. 12   14. 7   15. 365, 366
16. weeks   17. February   18. 4
19. No 20. 29   21. Answers shows one week circled   22. 4   23. Tuesday

p. 133: 1-10. Answers Vary   11. Merci
12. Gracias   13. Danke

p.134: 1. 6/7   2. 1/3   3. 1/2   4. 2/3
5. 1/2   6. 7/10   7. 4/19   8. 4/5
9. 2/11   10. 1/3   11. 1/3   12. 1/2
13. 1/2   14. 1/5   15. 1/3
16. 1,2,5,10   17. 1,2,3,6,9,18
18. 1, 2,4,5,10,20
19. 1,3,4,6,9,12,18,36   20. 5   21. 4
22. 10   23. 4   24. 10   25. 25

p. 135: 1. Answers Vary   2. 3,1,2

CONGRATULATIONS!

your name

Has completed
Summer Fit!

and is ready for Fourth Grade!

Parent or guardian's signature

THANK YOU FOR STAYING ACTIVE!

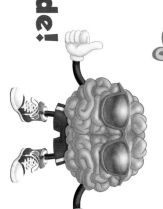